Clinical Interviews *with* Children *and* Adolescents

D1497522

Clinical Interviews *WITH* Children *AND* Adolescents

Philip Barker, MS, BS, FRCP(Ed.),
FRC Psych., FRCP(C)

*Professor of Psychiatry
and Pediatrics
University of Calgary*

W. W. NORTON & COMPANY

New York   *London*

Printed in the United States of America

First Edition

Library of Congress Cataloging-in-Publication Data

Barker, Philip.
  Clinical interviews with children and adolescents / Philip Barker.
  — 1st ed.
    p. cm.
  "A Norton professional book."
  Bibliography: p.
  Includes index.
  1. Interviewing in child psychiatry. I. Title.
  [DNLM: 1. Child Psychiatry. 2. Interview, Psychological – in
adolescence. 3. Interview, Psychological – in infancy & childhood.
4. Interview, Psychological – methods. WS 350 B255c]
RJ503.6.B37 1990   618.92'89 – dc19   89-16169

ISBN 0-393-70078-X

W.W. Norton & Company, Inc. 500 Fifth Avenue, New York, N.Y. 10110
W.W. Norton & Company Ltd., 37 Great Russell Street, London, WC1B 3NU

1 2 3 4 5 6 7 8 9 0

Goal: To bring a bright light of hope to a child.

To Thembi, Mellisa, and Christen

FOREWORD

It is a privilege to write the foreword to Professor Barker's latest book. *Clinical Interviews with Children and Adolescents* kindled in me memories of my sense of bewilderment when, as a trainee in child psychiatry, I was first exposed to my young patients.

Within minutes of his arrival in my small office, the restless five-year-old had climbed from the chair to my desk and was busy scattering my precious lecture notes across the floor. Aside from picking up the notes, how could I also establish rapport with David and save my office from destruction?

Later on, when on call, I wondered what I should say to the angry 13-year-old who was glaring at me from across the room. He had been brought to see the doctor who, he had been told, "will straighten you up." These experiences, common to every neophyte in the field, highlight the need for a "how to" description of the interviewing process by a sensitive and experienced clinician.

Techniques and styles must be tailored to the needs of those we are interviewing. This is crucial with children and adolescents who are developing rapidly – physically, cognitively, and emotionally. The interviewer's initial expression of interest in and concern for the child and the whole family will often be remembered as a fundamental ingredient of the ensuing therapeutic relationship. The amount of time involved in interviews may vary but the quality of the time must never be compromised. Careful and sensitive preparation will facilitate the progressive gathering of information.

Philip Barker, in a clear style that is easy to read, describes the basic principles of interviewing children. Suggestions derived from the author's experience abound. Examples include the provision of scented felt pens for younger children, the need to have both a "clean" and a "messy" play area, the importance of giving notice to the young person as the end of the interview approaches, how to handle the adolescent's coarse language or walking out of the room, the need for food or drinks during the interview, and the importance of a proper termination. Such tips are set against a thorough grounding in developmental psychology.

The second half of the book focuses on special clinical situations. How to interview physically and mentally handicapped children, the observation of infants, the tactful approach required for interviewing the abused child, and the challenge of the autistic child are all discussed with empathy and clinical acumen.

I wish this book had been available as I embarked upon my training.

Nady el-Guebaly, M.D., D.P.M., D.Psych.,
   F.R.C.P.(C), F.A.P.A, F.A.C.P.
Professor and Head
Department of Psychiatry
University of Calgary

CONTENTS

INTRODUCTION

This book is intended as a practical guide to interviewing children and adolescents in clinical settings. I hope it will be of help to students and practitioners in social work, health, psychology, and related fields.

Some of us are intuitively good at communicating with young people, while others have to work hard to acquire the necessary skills. All of us can, however, be more effective if we are aware of certain information on how to approach children of different ages and with different types of problem. My aim is to offer the reader such information.

While there are many objective and semi-objective tests that can be given to children of various ages, I have made only passing reference to these. Their uses and limitations are discussed in many texts on psychology and psychological testing. I have focused, instead, on the actual interview process. Nevertheless, much of the information in this book may be of help to those administering tests, questionnaires, and other structured material.

I have chosen to define the interview as a meeting of two people for exchange of information. An interview can of course involve more than two people. There may be more than one interviewer or more than one person being interviewed but I have concentrated on the one-to-one situation. When more than two people are involved, the basic principles are similar and the practical considerations only little different.

"Information", as used in the preceding paragraph, includes nonverbal as well as verbal messages. In many instances nonverbal material tells us more than the verbal. Indeed, some subjects are unwilling or unable to communicate verbally, but this does not mean they cannot be interviewed. Child psychiatrists and other professionals often meet non-speaking children. I hope this book will make it clear that it is not necessary to engage in two-way *verbal* interaction in order to interview them.

I have covered methods of interviewing children from infancy to late adolescence. I also discuss methods of approaching certain special groups of children, such as those who are psychotic, children with various handicaps, those who have been abused physically, sexually or emotionally, and those who may be suicidal. My colleague, Dr. Geoffrey Fisher, has contributed a chapter on interviewing mentally retarded children.

Although child psychiatry is my profession, this is not a book on the psychiatric assessment of children which I have discussed elsewhere (Barker, 1988; Barker, in press). The basic principles of establishing rapport with children, and then conducting interviews designed to obtain needed information are probably universal. While the information sought will vary from case to case, the approaches that are best used to obtain it are similar, be the interviewer a physician, social worker, psychologist, nurse, or health professional of another discipline.

What follows is thus a generic account of how to interview children. I hope that, whatever your clinical discipline, you will find in it something of practical help to you in your work.

ACKNOWLEDGMENTS

Many people have taught me what I know about interviewing children. Philip Connell was one of my earliest teachers, but many colleagues with whom I have subsequently worked have also taught me much, though they are too numerous to list. The many children and adolescents I have seen in my clinical practice have also been wonderful teachers. If young people do not like the way you meet, talk and play with them, they usually let you know, verbally or nonverbally, in no uncertain terms.

Of particular help to me in the preparation of this book was my colleague, Geoffrey Fisher. He has not only written one of the chapters, but also read and offered constructive comments on all the others. His input has made a real difference to the book. I am grateful also to Nady el Guebaly who kindly agreed to write the foreword, and for the support and encouragement he gave me while I was working on this book.

Barbara Hatt, librarian at Alberta Childrens Hospital, and her assistant Elisabeth Nielson, have, as always, been enormously helpful in obtaining the reference material I needed. The benefits of having a first class library service available when one is writing a technical book can hardly be overstated. In this respect I am singularly fortunate.

Finally I owe a debt of gratitude to Susan Barrows of W. W. Norton. For certain personal reasons I was unable to have the manuscript ready by the date originally agreed, and she has been most understanding and supportive of me over a difficult time in my life. It has been a real pleasure to work with her.

Clinical Interviews *with* Children *and* Adolescents

1

INTERVIEWING YOUNG
PEOPLE: SOME BASIC ISSUES

Clinical interviews with children may be conducted for many reasons. The form, content and tone will vary accordingly. Children are usually brought for interview by others and may have no particular desire to be interviewed. Sometimes it is the young person, usually an adolescent rather than a child, who requests the interview. This usually simplifies the process.

The following are some of the main situations in which clinicians may need to interview young people, though the list is not exhaustive.

(a) Mental health assessment. It is always necessary to interview a child during the process of assessing that child's psychiatric state. While the interview with the child is but a part of the assessment, it is a vital and central one. The emphasis is on the child's own internal mental processes and emotional state, although information about the child's family, school situation, relationships and social context is usually also sought. The specific information required, as well as the areas of inquiry which should be covered in such interviews, are spelled out in *Basic Child Psychiatry* (Barker, 1988).

(b) Psychological assessment. The interviews carried out

by psychologists in the course of their assessments of young people's clinical states have objectives similar to those of psychiatrists and other physicians who deal with children. In addition, clinical and educational psychologists are trained in the administration of psychological tests, which are often useful in supplementing the information obtained in "open-ended" interviews.

(c) Developmental assessment. The aim of some clinical interviews is primarily to assess a child's level of emotional, cognitive, or social development. While the child's developmental level is always important, the form of the interview may be different when the referring person(s)' concern is focused on developmental delay, either generally or in certain areas, from when other issues are the main focus of attention. Experienced clinicians can usually form accurate impressions of children's developmental levels. These may be supplemented by the administration of standardized tests. These tests are beyond the scope of this book.

(d) The investigation of abuse and neglect. Recent years have seen increasing recognition of the prevalence and importance of the physical, sexual and emotional abuse of children. Interviews with children who may have been abused, and sometimes with their siblings and peers, play a major role in the investigation of abuse or neglect. Special considerations that apply to such interviews are discussed in Chapter 9. The eliciting of facts and the obtaining of accurate information about what has been happening may be of particular relevance to the investigation.

(e) The facilitation of legal processes. Clinicians are increasingly being asked to interview children in connection with legal matters. These may be questions concerning the custody of children by divorced or separated parents, or access to their children by noncustodial parents. The increasing incidence of separation and divorce for the most part explains the rising demand for such interviews.

Assessment of children may be requested in the

resolution of other legal issues, which are alluded to briefly in Chapter 12.

(f) Dealing with emergency situations. The occasion to interview children sometimes arises in hospital emergency departments, clinics of various sorts, women's shelters, and other places where children are brought following some disaster or acute stress. Such interviews are usually focused on issues directly related to the emergency situation.

(g) Research. Many research projects in the fields of child development, child psychiatry and psychology, and social welfare involve interviews with children. These interviews are usually focused on particular issues and are structured to achieve the specific objectives of the research project concerned.

(h) Placement. Sometimes the primary goal of an interview is to make a decision regarding a child's placement in a living situation. Some children are unable, for various reasons, to live with their own families. In such cases the proper selection of alternative living situations is a matter of crucial importance. Interviews may be used to help in the selection of suitable alternative placements and to prepare children for life in a new home.

(i) Other situations. Interviews with children may be required in hospital wards, intensive care units, institutions of various sorts or, or many other places. In most of these cases the objectives are quite specific and the goals more limited than when a general assessment is being undertaken.

DEVELOPMENTAL CONSIDERATIONS

We must take developmental issues into account if our interviews with children are to be effective. Bierman and Schwartz (1986) summarize the situation well:

> Children perceive, conceptualize, and react to interpersonal events in characteristic ways depending

on their level of development. Their ability to conceptualize the motivations, feelings, and behaviors of themselves and others changes dramatically over time, along with their understanding of social causality and their ability to infer predictable patterns in their social world.

Children in their first few years of life think mainly in concrete terms and have not yet acquired the capacity for abstract thought. Their views and responses relate to their immediate situations and they are unable to view things from longer-term perspectives. Their vocabularies are also limited, hence they can often express themselves better through play or other indirect means.

As they approach and enter adolescence children become able to conceptualize things more as adults do and interviews with them can be conducted in ways which more closely resemble those which we use with adults.

Age is not the only consideration in deciding on the best approach to inteviewing a particular child. Children vary in their rate of development of cognitive functioning, ability to think in abstract terms and to view things in longer-term perspectives. Their social worlds and experience of life vary too. These issues must be taken into account.

THE CHALLENGE

Interviewing children and adolescents presents many challenges.

It is different from interviewing adults, and the younger the subject, the greater the difference. Following are some of the reasons for this:

1. Children's cognitive and language skills are less well developed than those of most adults, though their rate of development of such skills varies. Few things impede the development of rapport as much as talking

over the head of the person being interviewed. Talking at too simple a level can also be counterproductive.

2. Children are more often brought by others to be interviewed rather than coming of their own volition. It is usually their parents who bring them, and this sometimes helps reassure them. But many interviews are held at the behest of those outside the their families, such as child welfare authorities, teachers, the police or other professionals concerned with them.

    Some older children, especially adolescents, do come to be interviewed on their own initiative. This creates a rather different relationship between young person and interviewer from when the young person has been coerced or persuaded to come to the interview.

3. Young people are often interviewed because of their misdeeds, or alleged misdeeds. This may lead them to think that we are interviewing them to determine whether they have done what is alleged – or even to pass judgment on them in some way. While this is seldom the case, their perception can lead to suspiciousness or outright refusal to become actively involved in the interview process.

4. Many young people come ill prepared for the interview. In the course of my practice I have encountered children who have been told by their parents or, occasionally, others that I would be giving them "a good talking to" for their bad behavior, or that the interview with the psychiatrist was a sort of punishment for their misdeeds.

5. Many children, especially adolescents, have misconceptions about psychiatrists, psychologists, social workers and other mental health professionals. A common one is that the fact that you are to be interviewed by such a person implies that you are "crazy" or "insane," or at least that someone – perhaps your whole family – thinks so. Indeed, many people have fears of insanity and being told to see a psychiatrist or psychologist may serve to confirm such fears.

6. Communication difficulties are features of certain disorders which may affect children. Common examples are mental retardation, deafness, stuttering, and developmental language disorders. Less common ones are elective mutism and autistic disorders.

FLEXIBILITY

The above considerations dictate a need for a flexible approach to interviewing children. Fixed or rigid interview schedules do not work. The interviewer must, from the first contact, be alert to the feedback the child is offering, both verbal and non-verbal, with special emphasis on the latter. At every stage, you should adapt the way you handle the interview according to the responses you are getting. Remember that we do not have any absolute right to have our questions answered accurately – or indeed, at all. Nor is the there any fundamental reason why the child should draw a picture when we ask or play with the toys which we provide. To achieve these goals we must use our personal resources and our observations of the child's responses.

Every person who interviews a child naturally has an agenda – a list of things which the interview is intended to accomplish. Usually it is advisable to steer a middle course between following that agenda and accommodating to the child's present emotional state, responses, and wishes.

In the course of the interview it may emerge that some of the areas you wish to explore are sensitive ones. These can sometimes be anticipated. For instance it is reasonable to expect that children who have been in trouble with the law may not be overly keen to discuss their offenses, and those who are failing at school may be sensitive on the subject of school work and results. In such cases it is usually wise to leave such topics until late in the interview, unless they are first brought up by the child. Sometimes you might also find that children are sensitive in areas in which you had no reason to expect them to be. This should not only alert you to

the possible existence of problems which you did not suspect, but also warn you to tread carefully when exploring
these.

It is usually possible, through gentle probing, to discover
whether a child is ready to discuss a particular subject. If the
child is not, or you are in doubt, it is usually best to delay
raising the subject, perhaps even until a second or subsequent
interview. Important as it may be for us to obtain the information are seeking, we should respect the child's right to limit
discussion of particular topics or to withold information.

THE NEED FOR RAPPORT

Rapport is as hard to define as it is necessary for the
success of interviews. It is more than trust. It is a state of
understanding, harmony and accord. People who are in rapport with one another have a sympathetic relationship and
feel warmly towards each other. Hypnotherapists have long
been aware of the importance of rapport. They know that
failure to establish a sufficient degree of rapport is the principal cause of failure to induce hypnotic trance. Rapport has
been described as: . . . that peculiar relationship existing between subject and operator, wherein, since it [hypnosis] is a
cooperative endeavor, the subject's attention is directed to
the operator, and the operator's attention is directed to the
subject. Hence the subject pays no attention to externals or
the environmental situation (Erickson, Hershman, & Sector,
(1961), page 66).

This quotation describes well the involvement of hypno-
tist and hypnotic subject, but it does not emphasize the
positive and trusting feelings which underlie rapport. When
a high degree of rapport exists, each partner in the transac-
tions feels valued by the other. In clinical interviews this
means that those being interviewed feel that the interviewer
has their best interests at heart and cares enough to understand them and, in whatever way may be appropriate, to
help.

OPEN VERSUS CLOSED QUESTIONING

Rutter and Cox (1981) distinguish "open" from "closed" questions. An interview may aim to discover specific factual information, or it may be designed to explore, in a more tentative way, the emotional state, points of view, and opinions of a person. A police officer interviewing a witness to a motor vehicle accident is mainly concerned with the facts of the incident under investigation. For this purpose closed questions are generally best. On the other hand, a clinician interviewing a person who is emotionally upset is more concerned with that person's general emotional state and relationships. When talking to a patient for the first time, a clinician may have little information about the currently important issues in that person's life. In that situation open questions will probably be more useful.

Examples of "closed" questions include "Were the traffic lights at red when the car approached the intersection?" and "Was the driver signaling his intention to turn?" On the other hand, "Where would you like to start?" is an "open-ended" question; another is, "I wonder what's troubling you?" Open-ended questions give those being questioned the freedom to address a variety of issues. The police officer may be quite disinterested in what is on the subject's mind, being concerned only with establishing, as precisely as possible, what happened. The clinician is usually interested in both facts and feelings.

There are places for both closed and open questions in clinical interviews. In many circumstances it is best to start with an open-ended approach. The younger the child, however, the more necessary it is to use closed questions. Young children, especially preschoolers, may not be able to deal with questions such as, "Why have you come to see me?" If such a question is answered at all, the child's reply may be, "Because Mummy brought me," or something of that sort. The child is seldom the initiator of the interview and may have no specific agenda for it. In the early stages the interviewer should be more concerned with establishing rapport than with determining facts. It is generally better to start with some general exploration of the child's world. This is especially crucial if the child is very young.

We should keep in mind the relatively concrete thinking of young children when framing questions for them. If you ask a child, "What brought you here?" the answer may be, "A car." A request such as "Tell me about your family" is likely to be quite unproductive if addressed to a young child, whereas if used during an interview with an adolescent it might result in the client's revealing significant information. For younger children, more specific, closed questions are necessary. Examples are, "How many brothers or sisters do you have?" and "Will you tell me their names?" then perhaps, "Who do you play with the most?" For preschool children the latter would probably yield more information than "Who do you like the best?" since the latter is less concrete.

In due course closed questions will usually be necessary. For instance, often we *do* need to know whether the subject has ever contemplated, or attempted, suicide; if this proves to be the case it is important to obtain details of any self-destructive behavior that has occurred. As the subject is explored, specific, closed-ended questions will be needed so that the interviewer may have as precise an idea as possible of the risk of suicide. On the other hand, too many such questions in the early stages of an interview with an adolescent or even with an older prepubertal child may impede the establishment of rapport. It might cause important areas to be overlooked, because the the young person has not been given the opportunity to indicate these. Moreover an interview should not resemble an interrogation. It should be more like a conversation than a series of questions.

"Leading" questions imply that certain answers are expected. Examples include: "How long had the light been red when the motorist crossed it?" and "How often does your father hit you?"–when it has not been established that the motorist did cross the red light or that the father hits the child at all.

In framing questions and talking with children generally

it is important to balance prompting and encouragement. The interviewer's desire to obtain needed information may lead to excessive prompting, so that answers are almost put into the child's mouth.

SIMPLE VERSUS COMPLEX QUESTIONS

Simple questions are generally to be preferred to complex ones. Rutter and Cox (1981) distinguish, in addition to open and closed questions, "double" and "multiple choice" questions. Examples of double questions are, "Have you ever felt like killing yourself or running away from home?" or "Do you often get depressed or feel like crying?" It is best to divide such questions into two.

Multiple choice questions offer a number of possible answers. They can be useful in eliciting facts from subjects who are having difficulty communicating the information the interviewer wants, but they have limitations. The major problem is that one cannot include all the possible answers in the choice offered. But if a boy is having difficulty telling you how often he fights with his brother, questions like, "Does it happen once a day, once a week or less often than that?" may help give you some idea of the frequency of the incidents.

AN INTERVIEW IS A TWO-WAY HAPPENING

We must remember that an interviewer is giving information to the person being interviewed, as well as receiving it. This is the case whether we wish it or not. While we may not choose to give information about our personal lives, our appearance, manner, way of talking and reactions to what the person we are interviewing says all give us away. We should therefore always consider what we are communicating by such nonverbal means.

The issue of how much we wish to reveal about ourselves during clinical interviews also bears consideration. I have found that children, as well as parents, sometimes ask me questions such as whether I am married, whether I have children, and whether my children have caused me problems. There are various ways of dealing with such questions. A time-honored one among therapists is to turn the conversation to the reasons why the person is asking the questions. This may be discussed and, in some types of therapy, interpretations may be offered. Such an approach may not be appropriate in interviews which are not part of a process of therapy. I believe there is a place for self-disclosure, within limits, both in diagnostic and therapeutic interviews; however it is a personal matter for each clinician.

THE FUNCTIONS OF INTERVIEWS

Rich (1968) classified interviews into fact-finding, fact-giving, manipulative, treatment, and demonstrative types. These categories are not mutually exclusive, since more than one function can be served in an interview.

Fact-finding interviews are designed to discover information. In the clinical setting this may be historical data concerning the individual or family concerned or information about the subject's current condition or social setting. The interviewer may also be seeking insights into the subject's emotions, thought processes, and general mental state.

Fact-giving interviews are those in which the interviewer gives information to the person being interviewed. They are common in many nonclinical situations, as when employers or supervisors give their employees or subordinates instructions or data which they need for the performance of their duties. Press conferences and the interviews granted by politicians to journalists are other examples. In the clinical field, fact-giving may include telling clients the results of assessments, tests and other diagnostic procedures, explaining the nature of proposed treatment, and discussing options in the management of problem situations. Every initial interview should contain a fact-giving element, since those concerned need to know about the nature of the interview process, its confidentiality, the time frame and other relevant facts.

Manipulative interviews are those which impose change, or at least attempt to do so, on the person or persons interviewed. They are probably used rather rarely in clinical situations. The probation officer who tells a young person that, if he doesn't attend school regularly, or if she fails to observe her curfew, he will institute further court proceedings which might lead to incarceration, is in each case conducting a manipulative interview.

Treatment interviews do not impose change but aim to promote it. Rich (1968) divides them into supportive, counseling and insight-giving types. The general principles and many of the techniques discussed in this book are applicable to treatment interviews. Psychotherapy techniques themselves fall outside the scope of this book.

Demonstrative interviews are intended to illustrate points, techniques or clinical conditions to an audience. They may be used in teaching or for research purposes. They raise issues of ethics and confidentiality, issues to which those conducting such interviews need to pay particular attention.

SUMMARY

Children may be interviewed in various clinical situations. Common ones include mental health assessment, psychological evaluation, developmental assessment, investigation of possible abuse or neglect, the need to facilitate legal processes and emergency situations in hospitals or elsewhere. They may also be requested when placement of the child in a new living situation is necessary, and for research purposes.

Developmental considerations are important in determining the interview approach called for in each case. Children coming for interview may have various fears and misconceptions about what is to occur. Flexibility in conducting interviews is therefore essential. The establishment of rapport is a vital prerequisite to the main work of an interview.

The way questions are framed is crucial to the success of an interview. Leading questions, for instance, should generally be avoided, and questions should be as simple and brief as possible.

An interview is a two-way event and the impact of the interview on the child must at all times be considered.

2

SETTING OBJECTIVES FOR THE INTERVIEW

Clinical interviews, like most human endeavors, go better if they have clear and well-defined objectives. It is important to think about the following before an interview begins:

FOR WHOM IS THE INTERVIEW BEING CONDUCTED?

Children and adolescents are interviewed for many reasons. The initiative for the interview may come from someone else. When it does come from the child, the situation may be rather out of the ordinary. For instance, a 17-year-old boy whom I had seen on and off for several years, though not for the last 18 months, telephoned to ask if I would see him again. He said it was a private matter he could not discuss over the phone. Danny had been in the care of a child welfare agency for much of his life and had lived mainly in group homes and foster homes. When he came to my office it emerged that he wanted to talk to me about the difficulty he was having in dating girls. He didn't know how to set about asking a girl for a date and had a great fear that he would say or do the wrong thing and get rejected.

Danny had not told anyone he was coming to see me; the initiative for this interview was clearly his. Since the matter under discussion was a personal one, I did not have to consider or inform anyone else, even though Danny was still in the care of the child welfare agency. We were able to discuss his problem, in ways which he seemed to find helpful, in the course of two sessions.

Interview situations with children are seldom as simple as this. Usually a third party is involved, sometimes a fourth, a fifth or more. Hence the importance of asking who really wants the interview to take place—by no means always a simple question to answer.

WHAT IS THE WIDER CONTEXT OF THE INTERVIEW?

The relevant context for an interview will usually include the child's family situation, it will often include his or her school context, and if the young person is employed, the employer may be involved. Sometimes a child welfare agency, other social agencies, the police, the courts, youth organizations, or the neighborhood community may be involved in the child's life. The child's peer group is often important too. Any or all of these may be involved in the issues the interview is to address, and their interests and points of view may need to be taken into account. However, it will not always be appropriate to give priority to their interests or to accept their objectives as yours.

The others involved may have a variety of agendas and objectives. While they usually share the aim of helping the young person in some way, their ideas about how the interview should be conducted often differ. For instance, the parents may wish for a change in the child's behavior or school progress, while the child may be unconcerned about either of these things and may want more freedom of action. A juvenile court may wish primarily to understand the circumstances of an offense a young person has committed in order to make an appropriate disposition, while the young person's main concern may be to avoid conviction or to reduce the severity of the sentence.

Referrals from courts or interviews which may lead to

reports to courts present special problems. I have found that in such cases it is usually best to avoid asking questions bearing on the issue of whether the young person is guilty of the offense in question. It is for the court to determine issues of guilt or innocence, not those carrying out clinical assessments. My function is usually to assess the child's mental state, personality strengths and weaknesses, and developmental stage. (Different considerations apply when the referral is initiated to discover whether the young person is fit to stand trial, but young people are rarely referred for this purpose.)

WHAT INFORMATION IS TO BE OBTAINED DURING THE INTERVIEW?

A few minutes spent considering precisely what you want to learn will enable you to conduct a more focused and effective interview. While there is always a need to establish rapport and to get to know the child in a general way, it is helpful also to have a list of questions you want to be able to answer at the end of the interview. These may be almost infinitely varied. A few examples are:

Is the child depressed?

Is there a risk of suicide?

Has this young person been physically (or sexually) abused?

What are the causes or associated factors involved in the child's failure to perform adequately at school?

Is the young person abusing alcohol or other drugs?

Is there evidence of addiction to alcohol or other drugs?

Is the child in contact with reality or is there evidence of a psychotic process?

Is hypnotherapy (or another treatment method) likely to be helpful?

It can be helpful to write down the list of questions and check them off, mentally if not with a pencil, as they are dealt with during the interview.

WHAT WILL YOU DO WITH THE INFORMATION YOU OBTAIN?

This is an important question for it is related to the confidentiality of the interview. Occasionally, as in the case of Danny mentioned above, nobody needs to be informed of the outcome of the interview or told what information emerged during it. In my experience, however, this is rather unusual. Most children are referred by other professionals or are brought by their parents, and these people must be informed of the results of the interview. Nevertheless, the amount of detail they need be given concerning the content of the interview varies.

There are at least four categories of people to whom information may be passed:

The referring person.
The parents or guardian.
Courts or agents of the courts, such as probation officers or lawyers.
Other interested parties, such as teachers, the staff of child welfare services, or the police.

The referring person, when there is one, should always be informed of the outcome of the interview. The clinician must consider the amount of detail and the type of information that should be passed on. For example, the staff of a school that refers a child because of learning or behavior problems will probably require less detailed information about the dynamics of that child's family than would be needed by a family therapist. Moreover, families often do not wish their children's teachers to be given intimate details of their personal lives or problems; nor do teachers usually need to know of them.

The staff of a group home or treatment center may be interested primarily in questions such as whether the child presents a suicidal risk or is psychotic, and information which does not bear on these concerns may not need to be included in the report of the interview. Courts, too, usually have specific questions they want answered and are not concerned about other matters, even though these may be of interest to the clinician.

Local circumstances will often determine how much and what sort of information you will pass on to referral agencies. Knowledge of how well information passed on in confidence is indeed kept confidential by the social agencies, school systems, and other institutions you deal with will influence your behavior in this respect.

Parents and legal guardians are entitled to and should normally receive information concerning the interview. There will be occasional exceptions to this, for example where an emancipated adolescent is out of touch with his or her parents, or where the adolescent takes the initiative in setting up the interview—like the interview with Danny mentioned in Chapter 1. The information given will include at least a general opinion concerning the issues which the interview addressed. The extent to which the content of the interview will be discussed with the parents depends on circumstances, including the child's wishes in the matter.

Penfold (1987) has drawn attention to the benefits of "open reporting." She suggests that "there are many advantages to open communication with parents, having them present in conferences about their child and giving them copies of psychiatric reports." This issue will be discussed further in Chapter 12.

Courts and their agents usually require reports and information of a rather different type from that needed by most other referral sources. The various situations in which the input of psychiatrists and other mental health professionals may be requested for legal purposes are discussed more fully in Chapters 17 and 18 of *Basic Child Psychiatry* (Barker, 1988). We will also return to this subject in Chapter 12.

WHAT ARE THE LIMITS OF CONFIDENTIALITY THAT WILL APPLY TO THE INTERVIEW?

It is important to specify the limits of confidentiality to those you are interviewing and others involved. To do this you must be clear about them yourself.

There are two categories of information you may need to pass on after you have interviewed a child. The first is your opinion on questions concerning the child's condition. If the interview is concerned with mental health issues, questions such as "Is the child depressed?" or "Is there a risk of suicide?" or "Why is this child failing in school?" may be relevant. The second category consists of information about the content of the interview, that is, what the child actually told you or revealed in nonverbal ways such as play. Information of the first type usually needs to be passed on; that of the second type often does not. What *is* important here is that all concerned know what information is to be given to whom. This should be explained early in the interview. In my experience being open and frank about these matters usually helps establish trust and facilitates the interview process.

(An advantage of interviews with whole families, which are often a valuable means of obtaining information about children, though they are not the focus of this book, is that all concerned are present to hear everything that is said.)

When I first see them, I explain to children, parents and whole family groups, that the interviews I will be having with them are confidential. I explain that I make a record of each interview and assure them that information in it will not be communicated to others without their permission, though I also explain that I report my findings and recommendations to referring physicians — something to which children and their parents rarely object. If referral comes from someone other than a physician, for example a member of the staff of a school or social agency, I discuss with the person being interviewed what information should be sent to the referring person; if he or she wishes to limit this or to have no information passed on, I will respect his or her wishes.

While I make it clear, especially to older children and adolescents, that what they say will not normally be reported to their parents without their consent, I also tell them that there are some exceptions to this. The main one concerns things so serious that the parents must know about them. Examples I mention are suicide plans and the expressed intention of the child to run away. I explain that I cannot allow children to get into dangerous situations without their parents knowing about the possible dangers. I point out that I believe their parents wish to help them avoid such dangers.

Since in most jurisdictions there are legal requirements to report certain things, notably the various forms of child abuse, I also explain what these requirements are. I assure all concerned that I would inform them if I was going to make a report to the relevant authorities. This warning comes as part of a package which, I tell the family, I present to all the children and families I see. There is thus no implication that it applies more to the particular child or family I am seeing at the time, than to any other.

It is important to be aware of the law in the jurisdiction in which you practice. Each of the 50 United States and the 10 Canadian provinces has its own child welfare legislation; so do England and Wales, Scotland, Ireland, and many other countries. Definitions of abuse vary and the circumstances in which suspected abuse must be reported are defined differently. In some jurisdictions the law is more rigid in its definitions than in others; phrases like 'reasonable grounds to suspect' often occur, leaving scope for interpretation of what is reasonable.

When I find myself in a position where I must make a report to the child welfare authorities, I usually also offer to act as the family's advocate, for example, by letting the authorities know that the family is engaged in therapy with me and is making progress, if this is the case; if it is not, the family almost invariably has strengths and assets to which attention can be drawn. If I am able and willing to continue therapy with the family, I make this clear also.

In these often difficult situations it is essential to keep those you are interviewing or treating fully informed. While few like having their cases brought to the attention of child welfare authorities, many understand why this is necessary once it is explained.

HOW MUCH TIME IS AVAILABLE FOR THE INTERVIEW? WILL IT BE POSSIBLE TO ARRANGE FURTHER INTERVIEWS?

In an ideal world one would have as much time as necessary to interview every child one has to see. In reality this is not so. Some of the factors that may constrain the time available include the interviewer's schedule, that of the child or family, the deadline for a report (as is often applied to interviews conducted for courts), and economic factors, particularly the financial resources of those paying for the services being provided.

The interviewer should know how much time is likely to be available for the interview and should share this information with the person interviewed. Not only does this often help focus the interview so that both can work to get the task completed in the time available, but it also means that the child is not surprised or disappointed when the time to finish comes.

A related question is whether it will be possible to conduct further interviews with the young person. If it is, the gathering of information becomes less urgent and more time can be spent establishing rapport. It may also be less necessary to get quickly to the major issues that have to be addressed. When time is limited, some compromise has to be made between spending adequate time establishing rapport and obtaining needed information.

IF FURTHER CLINICAL WORK WITH THE YOUNG PERSON IS NEEDED, WILL YOU BE ABLE TO CARRY THIS OUT?

Some interviews are single clinical encounters or part of what is known to be a brief assessment for a specific purpose. Others may be the start of a long-term therapeutic, counseling or other professional relationship. When we know that it is possible that the interview may be part of a longer-term relationship, we should discuss this at the beginning of the interview. We should consider also whether we will be in a position to carry out further work with the child should this prove to be necessary, and should give this information to the person we are interviewing.

If the interview is one of a series, perhaps designed to achieve some therapeutic purpose, this fact should be established at the outset so that it will be known to all parties.

OTHER POINTS CONCERNING OBJECTIVES

Whatever the objectives of an interview with a young person, they should be expressed in positive terms. I have discussed the setting of therapeutic objectives at greater length elsewhere (Barker, 1986, Chapter 6); similar principles apply even when the objectives are not primarily therapeutic. The basic points are:

1. Objectives should be expressed in positive terms. Rather than aiming to stop a behavior, for example, they should define the behavior(s) that should replace what is not desired.

2. The context(s) in which change is desired should be defined. Most, maybe all, behaviors are of value in some circumstances. The child who invents elaborate and ingenious stories when accused of theft or other misdeeds may have a valuable skill that could be applied to the writing of short stories or other sorts of fiction. There are appropriate circumstances for the display of anger or sadness, even though one aim of therapy may be to help the subject overcome this in other situations.

3. Changes desired should be operationally defined. Terms like "being happy" or "getting along better with" someone are too vague to be of much value. The definitions should be more precise than that. For example, rather than saying that siblings should get along better, a preferable phrasing of the objective might be that they would be able to play together

happily without getting into fights and would converse in friendly terms rather than calling each other names.

4. The interviewer should be wary of requests to find out the "why" of something. Questions like "Why am I feeling depressed?" or "Why is my child behaving in this way?" do not lend themselves to definitive answers. They are often based upon the assumption that the answers will lead to solutions. While this is so in many branches of natural science, including medicine, in social sciences it is often not the case and clear-cut, unitary causes are the exception. The clinical problem that presents itself is liable to have multiple causes, some of them dating back far into the past—for example, into the childhoods of the parents of the child you are interviewing.

   While understanding what we can of causation is much to be desired, it is a mistake to permit our patients and clients to assume that a quick solution will result from the elucidation of causes. Moreover, it is often hard to be sure about the causation of behavioral and emotional problems. Requests to discover the causes of disorders are usually veiled requests for change. It is better to specify the desired outcome, rather than agreeing to seek for causes.

5. Are there any potential drawbacks to the stated objectives? Sometimes things take on a less desirable countenance when examined more closely. Consider, for example, the anorexic adolescent girl whose symptoms are associated with a specially close relationship to her mother. The latter may spend much of her time and energy in efforts to help her daughter overcome her eating problem. The resolution of the problem might mean that much of the closeness between mother and daughter would be lost— a possible drawback.

   Sometimes it is necessary, for the resolution of a child's problem behavior, for a parent—it may be the father—to become more involved in the life of the family. That, in turn, might mean that he must spend less time at his work, which could lead to a lowering of the family's income. Whether this "trade-off" is worthwhile is something which should be considered when the objectives are discussed.

6. What consequences will follow once the objectives are met? This question is similar to the preceding one but offers another way of looking realistically at the merits of the objectives under discussion.

7. What has stopped the person, family or group from making the changes now desired?

8. How quickly do those concerned wish to achieve their objectives? Since change can create a need for big adjustments in people's lives, the fastest possible pace of change is not always the best. Asking this question has the additional merit that embedded in it is the message that change *will* occur. The issue becomes one of when change will occur, not whether it will.

SUMMARY

Clinical interviews should have well-defined objectives. It is important to establish on whose behalf the interview is being conducted. The interviewer should also be clear about the wider context of the interview, the information which he or she hopes to obtain, what is to be done with the information obtained, the limits of the confidentiality of the interview, the time available, and whether any follow-up work will be possible should it be needed.

Objectives should be operationally defined and stated in positive terms. The context(s) in which changes are desired should be defined. Attempting to answer "why" questions is generally unhelpful; objectives are better stated in terms of changes desired. Any possible drawbacks to the changes requested should be considered, together with the factors that have previously stood in the way of change.

3

PREPARATIONS AND RAPPORT BUILDING

Careful preparation for an interview pays dividends. The preliminary contacts with the child and the family should have a positive, optimistic tone. The interviewer must come to the interview prepared and provide suitable physical surroundings and sufficient time for the interview, so that things are not rushed. Careful attention to these matters facilitates the establishment of rapport and increases the chances of success for the interview.

THE PHYSICAL SURROUNDINGS

Many clinical interviews are conducted in offices, therapy rooms or playrooms designed specifically for the purpose. When this is so the interviewer starts with an advantage. Sometimes it is necessary to conduct interviews in places not designed for the purpose or in rooms which have multiple uses. Some improvisation is then necessary.

Comfortable physical surroundings help set the tone of the interview. They are important in the waiting room area as well as in the place where the child is to be seen. The interview room should be pleasantly furnished, well ventilated, and unobtrusively lit. Comfortable chairs of sizes suitable for the child or children to be seen, paper tissues (in case of tears), and toys and other child-oriented items should be provided. The surroundings should be child-centered, and the age of the child to be interviewed should be taken into account. Adolescents may not feel comfortable in a room furnished for young children. While it is seldom feasible to have multiple rooms designed for use by children of different ages, it is often possible to have items suited to the needs of children of different ages or levels of development in different areas of a room.

A well-designed child interview room has cupboards or other readily accessible storage space, so that items not likely to be needed by particular children can be stored out of sight. If a child asks for something that is not in view but is available, it can quickly be retrieved, provided, of course, that the interviewer wishes to accede to the child's request.

The following items should be available in a child interview room:

- A table of regular height, with paper, writing and drawing materials (I have found that many younger children have a particular liking for scented felt pens), an eraser, and a ruler. There should be at least two chairs, one for the child and one for the interviewer. I prefer to have a table big enough to enable me to sit beside, rather than opposite, the child.
- A lower table of suitable height for preschool children, with chairs to match. This also should be provided with paper and drawing materials. An alternative is to have, along one wall of the room, a Formica-topped working surface of suitable height, open underneath so that child and interviewer can sit comfortably at it. The working surface might be of regular table height in one part of its length and of "preschool" height in another.
- An easel with a ledge for paints, brushes and water. Protective aprons for children to wear while painting should be provided. Some parents do not take kindly to being presented, at the end of the interview, with a child whose clothes are covered with paint.

- A dollhouse, furnished and equipped with family fig- ures representing adults and children of different ages and both sexes.
- A sand tray, with a supply of toys available nearby. These may include toy animals, human figures, vehi- cles, and fencing (of the type used on farms). Some like to have water available so that it can be mixed with the sand to form mud, but this can present practical diffi- culties.
- A supply of toys, building blocks, "Lego," board games, "Plasticine," and puppets. A variety of puppets is desir- able. Some should be animal figures; others should be human ones. Characters from TV shows, such as "Muppets," are often particularly acceptable to young children. Both glove puppets and face puppets should be available. The "human" puppets should include both white and black ones, and if children of oriental or other ethnic groups are among your clientele, these should be represented also.
- Most of these items may be kept in cupboards or on shelves and made available at the interviewer's discre- tion. Having too many play materials in view and ac- cessible can be a mistake, especially if they are items not suited to the age of the child being interviewed. If they arouse too much interest in the child this may interfere with the progress of the interview.
- A bookshelf carrying a small selection of books suit- able for children of different ages. These may be used to engage children's interest, to assess their attitudes towards reading matter, or to obtain rough-and-ready estimates of their reading skills.
- A sink with running water and a draining board. This can be used as a water supply for painting and as a pond for floating boats or drowning unloved figures or animals.

There is much to be said for arranging the room so that each group of items is in a distinct area. The attention of the children interviewed can thus be directed to those areas likely to be of interest to them, though others are available to children who prove to be more or less mature than the interviewer expected, or for those who express special interest in particular items. Older children can be told that the area where the younger children's items are need not concern them, and vice versa.

It is a good idea, if space permits, to have "clean" and "messy" play areas, perhaps with a room divider or partial wall in between. The "clean" area will contain the books, board games, writing and drawing materials, "Lego," building blocks and so forth, while the "messy" area houses the sink, the sand tray, modeling clay, and painting materials; the latter should have a waterproof, washable floor, while the clean area may be carpeted, though in that case a rugged, readily cleaned carpet is desirable.

Adolescents, especially older ones, are usually best seen in an office suitable for adults. An ideal arrangement is to have the office adjacent to the child-oriented interview room (which may be referred to as the playroom, a term which has positive connotations for most children), with an intercommunicating door. It is then possible to move from one to the other if necessary. Some adolescents, for example, prove to be quite immature, in terms of their emotional or cognitive development. Therefore we can expect to learn more from interviewing them in a playroom than in an office appropriate to their chronological age.

PREPARING CHILD AND FAMILY

The preparation for the interview starts with the first contact between you, or whoever may be acting on your behalf, and the child or, more probably, a parent. If it consists of a telephone conversation, a secretary, receptionist or other professional colleague who takes the call should be familiar with your way of working and able to answer basic questions the caller may have. Such people should be aware of the limits to the information they can give out and be clear about what they should tell callers about the referral procedure and related matters.

While the content of the conversation will depend on the circumstances and the nature of the clinician's practice, certain universal rules apply. For instance, callers should find themselves speaking to someone who is both courteous and knowledgable.

The importance of the first contact can hardly be exaggerated. For many people, making contact with a mental health professional or other clinician is both difficult and anxiety-provoking. It may bring to the fore feelings of guilt and other strong emotions. Many parents feel responsible for their children's problems and the resulting guilt may be manifested in anxiety, defensiveness or undue sensitivity. They may in reality have been blamed by others, professionals as well as nonprofessionals.

When children will be interviewed by a clinician in the mental health field, they or their parents may fear that the child—or perhaps even the parent—is "crazy" or suffering from some major mental problem. While this may of course be the case, in many instances the worst fears of parents and their children prove not to be justified. Whatever the facts of the case eventually turn out to be, the person involved in the initial contact should be aware of how clients may feel when they are making contact with clinicians and should be supportive and empathic, as well as well informed.

The caller's anxiety may also be related to the reluctance many people feel about revealing what they consider personal or sensitive information to a stranger. They wonder if they can trust the interviewer and what he or she will think of them when they speak of their problems and tell their personal history. The confidential nature of the interviews that may follow should therefore be stressed when such issues arise or appear to be of concern to the caller.

Telephone contact by the clinician or a secretary or receptionist is not always possible, in which case the necessary preparatory information may be sent in a letter or by way of the referring professional, if there is one. The referrer can sometimes provide much of the preliminary explanation and reassurance to the child and family. This applies if that person is your colleague and is familiar with the service you provide and with your way of working. This is more often the case in small communities than in large metropolitan areas.

ARRIVAL AT THE CLINIC OR OFFICE

When the child and any accompanying adult(s) arrive they should be made to feel expected and welcome. The receptionist or secretary should be aware of who is coming, including the names of the children in the family, so that all can be greeted by name.

If the initial contacts have proceeded satisfactorily, child and family will have some idea of what is to happen. The person greeting them should also be able to give them any preliminary information they may not have received or have forgotten, as well as explaining anything they have not fully understood.

A child-oriented waiting area with toys, play materials, and reading matter suitable for children of all ages helps put families at ease. It is not necessary to have large quantities of toys, but there should be something for everyone.

We should try to obtain any necessary identifying or other information while the child and family are waiting. If there is a possibility that the start of the interview will be delayed beyond the scheduled time, those waiting should be told and an explanation given; however, the interviewer should try to be punctual and to avoid delays.

PREPARATIONS BY THE INTERVIEWER

Advance preparation usually makes for a better interview. I find it helpful, immediately before the interview, to review any referral or other background information that is available to me, even though I have read it before. If the interview is not the first, I like to refresh my memory by looking over my notes of previous sessions, especially the last one or two. Any drawings or other artwork that were left unfinished at the last session should be retrieved and ready for completion at this one.

Ensuring that the full time period scheduled for the interview is available and that your schedule is not overbooked will enable you to start on time and will ensure that you do not have to rush the interview. In many types of clinical practice it may, on occasion, prove impossible to achieve these objectives because of emergency situations and other crises. In such cases, the child and family should always be given an explanation and apology. You will often find that your clients are glad to know that you attend promptly to those in crisis or faced with unforeseen emergencies.

It will sometimes be impossible to meet all these recommendations when carrying out unscheduled interviews, especially those conducted in emergency situations and away from your office or home base. Efforts to meet them as far as is possible should nevertheless be made.

ESTABLISHING RAPPORT

The preceding preparatory measures will have set the stage for the establishment of rapport. They help ensure that children and their families arrive for interviews in a positive frame of mind. They make it more likely that the child will have pleasant expectations of the interview.

Establishing rapport has been given various names. Karpel and Strauss (1983) refer to "building working alliances" and Minuchin (1974), in *Families and Family Therapy*, describes the process as "joining" families. As rapport develops the participants become increasingly involved with each other. Once it is well established an interviewer or therapist can say almost anything, even quite outrageous things, without causing offense; remarks that might be construed as insulting will be taken as being meant jokingly or at least not seriously.

Rapport may be fostered by both verbal and nonverbal means. The nonverbal ones are probably the more important. A warm, friendly tone of voice, and a respectful, interested and accepting approach are important. I like to greet the child I am to interview, and any accompanying family members or other adults, in the waiting room. If I know their names, I will address each family member by name and shake hands with each (except for very small children); if I do not know their names I ask for them as I greet them. I tell the family who I am and express my pleasure at their arrival.

Although there is a lack of hard data on this, I believe that an interviewer's physical appearance and mode of dress affect, at least to some extent, the establishment of rapport. While your clothing should conform to cultural norms, overly formal dress can cause some children to feel ill at ease, as can the white coats that physicians and other personnel tend to wear in hospitals.

In establishing rapport the most important factor of all is the interviewer's behavior. Excellent rapport can be established virtually anywhere—in classrooms, public parks, prison cells, or on the beach. Rapport is promoted by matching or "pacing" the behavior of the person you are interviewing. You can do this by matching that person's postures and movements, respiratory rhythm, speed of talking, and voice tone and volume. You can also "mirror" or "cross-match" their movements; mirroring is the moving of, say, your left arm or leg in rhythm with similar movements of your client's right arm or leg. "Cross-matching" occurs, for example, when you move your hand or finger in rhythm with movements of the subject's foot. You may also choose to match movements such as the crossing and uncrossing of the legs, tilting the head to one side or the other, and leaning forward or settling back.

Pacing should be done sensitively and unobtrusively. It is only necessary to match some of the behaviors of the person you are interviewing; you do not need to behave like a robot. If you follow these guidelines, those you are interviewing will not become consciously aware that you are pacing them. Dilts, Grinder, Bandler, and DeLozier (1980, pages 116–117) point out:

> When you pace someone – by communicating from the context of their model of the world – you become synchronized with their own internal processes. It is, in one sense, an explicit means to "second guess" people or to "read their minds," because you know how they will respond to your communications. This kind of synchrony can serve to reduce resistance between you and the people with whom you are communicating. The strongest form of synchrony is the continuous presentation of your communication in sequences which perfectly parallel the unconscious processes of the person you are communicating with – such communication approaches the much desired goal of irresistibility.

You can also use your verbal communications to promote rapport. It is helpful to match your predicates with those used by whomever you are interviewing (Bandler, Grinder, & Satir, 1976; Bandler & Grinder, 1979). Predicates are verbs and the words used to explain actions or conditions, that is, mainly adjectives and adverbs. Some people use mainly visual, rather than auditory or feeling, predicates – as in the phrases, "I see what you mean," or "Things are looking brighter."

Sentences such as "I hear what you're saying," "That sounds terrible," or "It was like music to my ears," illustrate the use of auditory predicates. "Kinesthetic" or feeling-type predicates are used in sentences such as, "I have a lot of heavy problems", "That feels like a good idea," or "That's a weight off my mind." Although we all use predicates of all three types – as well as some olfactory ("This business smells fishy to me") and gustatory ("It leaves a bad taste in my mouth") ones, and many that are nonspecific, most of us have a preferred way of processing information, which is usually one of the three main sensory channels. Noting individuals' preferred processing mode and using the information to "join" them is a powerful rapport-building technique.

As well as matching predicates, you should listen carefully to the vocabularies of those you are interviewing, noting the words and expressions they use. Few things impede the establishment of rapport as much as repeatedly using words and expressions which are unfamiliar to those with whom you are speaking. This is especially true when dealing with children, since their vocabularies vary enormously. Age, level of cognitive development, educational attainment and sociocultural factors all affect children's use and knowledge of words.

Other useful rapport-building devices are:

- Accepting the views of those you are interviewing without challenging them, at least initially. This does not necessarily mean that you agree with or approve of the views expressed, but that you respect the right of the person you are interviewing to hold them. Sometimes it may be helpful to ask the young person to tell you more about his or her views or otherwise to indicate that you wish to understand his or her position more fully.
- Adopting a "one-down" position. The "one-down" position is the reverse of the authoritative, knowledgable stance expected of us by many of those we see in the course our clinical work. Many people are overawed or feel intimidated by "experts." Children, in particular, may come to us in such a frame of mind. By taking a "one-down" approach we can help counter this. In interviewing a child a "one-down" device might be to ask the child, from a position of ignorance, about something in which the child has expertise and you do not — skateboarding, video games or television cartoons perhaps, or how to spell his or her name. Expressing puzzlement and asking the child to help you out by explaining something can be helpful.
- Talking of experiences and interests you have in com-

mon with the person you are interviewing. These might be hobbies, sports, interests or pastimes you have in common with the child. Other possible areas of common experience are having lived in the same city, country, province or state as the child has in the past, or having visited the same places. The range of possible common experiences is almost infinite.

RAPPORT AS A CONTINUING STATE

The development of rapport is not a separate or specific part of the interview but a continuing process which should last as long as you have a professional relationship with the person concerned. It can always be developed further; the reverse is also possible. Although it is certainly true that once it is well established rapport can withstand a lot of stress, it nevertheless can be damaged or even destroyed at any time if continuing attention is not paid to maintaining it.

DEALING WITH FEELINGS AROUSED WHEN INTERVIEWING CHILDREN

Children's behavior, appearance and conversation may arouse a wide variety of feelings in those interviewing them. Some children are friendly, happy and engaging; others are hostile, sullen and resistant to one's attempts to engage them; some are flirtatious; others withdrawn and uncommunicative; sometimes "passive aggression," the negativistic refusal to cooperate without the open expression of aggression, may predominate. In some cases revelation of the child's present predicament or past experiences – as of physical, sexual or emotional abuse – may arouse particularly strong feelings in the interviewer. Some forms of child abuse can be truly horrifying, and learning of them can sorely tax the emotional resources even of those experienced in this field.

Those who choose to work with troubled children must be prepared for all of the above. Being prepared is indeed the first line of defense. It is not that we shouldn't experience strong emotions when encountering particular clinical situations. On the contrary, if we lose our human compassion and our capacity to understand and empathize, we are likely to become ineffective as clinicians. Yet we must always examine our emotional reactions and consider whether they are affecting adversely the way we are working with any particular child or family. Expressing our concern for the child's predicament, acknowledging the child's anger, despair or sense of worthlessness, and reacting in constructive and supportive ways are generally to be desired. On the other hand, we must not be overwhelmed by the emotions aroused in us, nor must we allow them to affect our clinical judgment.

An occupational hazard for all who work with disturbed and especially abused children and their families, is the danger of identifying with the child against the parents or other caregivers. It is well to bear in mind that even parents who grievously abuse or injure their children are doing the best they can with the emotional, personality and instrumental resources available to them at the time. It may well be that they have themselves been abused or neglected as children and they lack the internal resources to function well as parents.

When you are dealing with clinical situations which arouse strong feelings of any sort, consultation with colleagues can be invaluable. You should not hesitate to discuss your feelings with a trusted colleague. The mere act of expressing how you feel to another person may help you obtain a more objective view of the situation. In addition, the counsel of a wise and experienced colleague can lighten the burden of dealing with these cases and may open up for you new possibilities in their management.

SUMMARY

Whenever possible children should be interviewed in suitably equipped rooms. Younger children are best seen in playrooms with a supply of toys and materials suited to their age. Preparation for the interview should include the provision of advance information about what is to happen to both child and parents.

Careful attention to the establishment of rapport should be a main initial focus. Verbal and especially nonverbal means of achieving this are available. "Joining" the child and accepting the child's point of view rather than challenging it are important in the early stages.

Those interviewing children must be prepared for the likelihood that some children, through their behavior, conversation, appearance, and especially their history of abuse or neglect, will arouse strong emotions in them. Examining these emotions and dealing with them appropriately are essential prerequisites to good clinical practice. The assistance and support of a network of professional colleagues can be invaluable in achieving this.

4

THE STRUCTURE AND STAGES
OF AN INTERVIEW

Most interviews have at least three stages: an introductory one, an information-seeking or information-giving one, and a termination stage. These stages, which might also be described as processes, are not mutually exclusive and may overlap. The building and maintenance of rapport are common to all three but are especially important during the first stage. In addition, it it is often necessary to obtain additional information from parents and others.

A clinical interview should be nonthreatening and nonjudgmental. At the outset the interviewer should accept the points of view, opinions, and emotional state of the person being interviewed. It is desirable to have a framework and structure in mind but flexibility and responsiveness to the reactions of the subject as different topics are discussed are also important. While in therapeutic interviews it is sometimes appropriate to challenge or confront, this does not mean denying the views or beliefs of the subject.

STRUCTURING THE INTERVIEW

I find it helpful to have the above stages in mind, especially when embarking on an initial interview. These stages or components may be used as a flexible outline of how to proceed. It is always important to be sensitive to the feedback the young person is giving you. Children may become anxious or defensive, or they may burst into tears when certain subjects are mentioned. Other subjects may be obvious sources of pleasure or delight. It is not always possible to anticipate what reaction particular subjects may provoke, but the child's reaction may be revealing and may tell you more than the verbal answers reveal.

Whenever you have prior information about a child's problems—and I find I almost invariably have some—this should alert you to which subjects may be sensitive ones. Thus, if the child is known to be in difficulty in school, it may be best to delay the exploration of issues related to school until rapport is well established. On the other hand, if the problem is thought to lie in the home and the child does well at school, it may be a good idea to discuss school issues early in the interview.

Many children are referred to mental health professionals because of behavior problems. They may have been subjected to criticism and punishment because of their behavior. They may therefore expect to be criticized or lectured when you interview them. Some are even told they are going to see someone "who will give you a good talking to," or "will find out why you're such a bad kid." Preparing children for interview in this way does not help but it sometimes happens. In such cases it is usually advisable to avoid getting quickly into a discussion of the "bad" behavior or associated topics. Even when children raise such issues themselves early in the interview, I may play them down and say that I would prefer to leave them until later. I might indicate that it is more important for me to get to know the young person first. This helps convey the point that I am not concerned simply with discussing the details of the child's misdeeds, and that I am concerned about his or her well-being. We must make it clear that we are not agents of punishment or disapproval, but are there to understand and help.

There are some exceptions to the principle that one should avoid the presenting problems until later in the interview. When the referral is initiated, or at least strongly desired, by the young person, it may be best to get quickly to the reason why help is being sought. This happens more often with adolescents than with prepubertal children, but the latter sometimes have symptoms (such as fears, pains or other physical symptoms) which are causing them concern and of which they wish to be rid. To brush such symptoms aside, saying that you will talk about them later, may give the impression that you are unconcerned with what is worrying the young person and have some other agenda.

It may sometimes be appropriate to acknowledge the areas of concern, to make it clear that one's main aim is to help with these matters, and to add a statement such as, "That must be a big worry to you and I'd like to hear all about it from you in a moment or two, but first I'd like to get to know you a little better." With an older adolescent this might be phrased in more "adult" terms, for example, "Obviously that's what you're mainly concerned about, but I'll be better able to help you with it if I can first get a little information from you about your background and your life in general. Then we'll return to what truly bothers you."

Sensitive issues may come up when the objectives of the interview are discussed. And when they do, we can acknowledge them, but do not have to go into them in depth. When the initiative for the interview comes from the young person, it usually takes some discussion of the presenting problems, which may be sensitive issues for the child, to clarify and determine the common objectives of the interview. In such cases you may agree that the aim is to work towards resolving the problems, but should leave in-depth discussion of them or speculation about their causes until later.

The above considerations call for a flexible approach. Best results come from going with the child's interests and being sensitive to the child's responses to your questions, suggestions and behavior. This does not mean that we should give children complete freedom to do exactly as they wish. As rapport develops, it usually becomes increasingly easy to direct the course of the interview. It *does* mean that the selection of topics to be discussed at particular points in the interview is governed in part by the child's responses. Meanwhile, there are usually certain issues which must eventually be addressed, regardless of the child's reactions.

At some point in the interview, usually when rapport is well developed, it may be helpful to give the child instructions, or forbid a certain activity of the child, in order to observe the response. Some children are charming and beautifully behaved until they are crossed or denied their way, whereupon there are dramatic changes in their demeanor and behavior.

Some children, especially younger ones whose language skills are at an early stage of development, prove to be poor conversationalists. This may be a signal that communication through play or other nonverbal means should be emphasized. The relative use you will make of verbal and nonverbal communication is another area where a sensitive and flexible approach is needed.

THE STAGES OF AN INTERVIEW

We have seen that interviews tend to consist of a series of stages; these usually overlap and the boundaries between them may be blurred.

Stage 1 is an introductory phase during which the participants make themselves known to each other. It may include exchange of pleasantries, and of basic identifying information (names, addresses, ages, position, affiliation and so on) if this is not already available, and a brief discussion of the tasks to be addressed during the interview. During this part of the interview you might wish to inquire about the child's age, birthdate, school attended, school grade, and job, if he or she has some part-time or after-school employment. I often tell the child a few things about myself: my name if the child does not already know it, my profession, the work I do, who has asked me to see him or her, and my understanding of the purpose of the interview.

A crucial part of the first stage, as mentioned in Chapter 3, is building rapport. While the building and maintenance of rapport should be continuing processes, starting even before the interview commences, it is during this stage the interviewer's primary concern. Much of the early parts of many interviews, especially first ones, is devoted primarily to rapport-building, the content of the interview taking second place.

Stage 2 essentially consists of exchange of information. In many clinical interviews the gathering of information is the focus, but sometimes the main business may be to give information to the person being interviewed. This is true when a clinical assessment has been completed and the results must be communicated to child and/or parents. Much exchange of information also occurs in the course of most psychotherapeutic interviews.

It is advisable to proceed to the information-exchanging stage only when adequate rapport has been established. When time constraints exist, this can present the interviewer with difficult decisions. A compromise sometimes has to be made between the need to achieve good rapport and the necessity of obtaining certain information within a limited time. Fortunately it is often possible to work on the development of rapport while exploring issues which are likely to be relatively nonthreatening.

Stage 3 is the termination phase. I like to give notice when the end of an interview is approaching. Warnings at ten or, at the latest, five minutes before the end of a session enable the young person to be prepared and to bring up anything he or she wishes before it is too late.

Part of the termination process should consist of putting the interview in context. If it is intended to be the first of a series, the interviewer's concluding remarks should look forward to the next one. This may involve setting the date and time, unless these are to be arranged after the interivew. If there is unfinished business, that is to say topics which were not definitively or fully discussed, the possibility of returning to them at the next session may be mentioned.

If the interview is to be the only one you will have with the child, some words of appreciation to the young person for sharing something of herself or himself are in order. I rarely interview anyone without learning something or being in some way enriched or (I hope) made wiser. I therefore like to thank the young person for this opportunity to learn something more of the human condition (though I do not word it in those terms!). Much the same applies if the interview is the last of a series, though in that case at least a few words summarizing the course of the treatment or assessment process are usually appropriate.

Perhaps the most important part of the termination phase of an interview is clarifying with the person you are interviewing what is to happen next. If you will be communicating with someone about your contacts with the child (for example, the referrer, the family, the school or another agency), you should mention this.

RAISING TOPICS AND ASKING QUESTIONS

Interviews with children and adolescents should not be interrogations. It can be tempting to ask a lot of questions, and it is necessary to ask some; however, more information is often obtained in less direct ways. You should use words familiar to the child, and your manner should be suited to the child's age and personality.

Asking direct questions may fail to yield the desired results. Rather than asking, "Do you dream at night?"or saying, "Tell me about your dreams!" try something like: "Lots of people have dreams when they are asleep at night . . . I wonder if you do?" The child who admits to having dreams can then be invited to recount one, and then perhaps asked whether the dreams are mostly nice ones or nasty ones. You might then say to the child who denies having or remembering dreams, "Often when people who don't have dreams come to see us, they like to make up a dream . . . to pretend they've had one . . . perhaps you'd like to do that?"

Having children make up dreams is one way of exploring their fantasy lives. Another is to ask them to imagine they can have three wishes and that "by magic" whatever they wish will come true; what would they most like to see happen? Children often take their wishes very seriously. Adolescents tend not to respond so well to questions phrased in terms of "magic" results. Simply asking them what "changes" they would like to see, without being any more specific than that, is often a more productive approach. Surprisingly revealing information sometimes emerges when children give their wishes. You may then go on to say something like, "Now perhaps you would like to pretend you were all alone on a desert island (or in a boat) and you could choose one person to be with you . . . anyone you like, but just one person . . . I wonder who you would have?" The child may then be asked to choose a second person, then a third.

Similar approaches can be used to inquire about fears, worries, and somatic and other symptoms ('Some people have things that make them feel frightened. I wonder if you have any?'). Conversation about family, friends (whom the child can be asked to name and describe), and school should be encouraged. Throughout all of this you should respond appropriately, sharing the child's sorrow at the loss of a pet, or pleasure at being a member of a winning sports team ("Wow, it must have been exciting beating that team!"). Above all, we must convey interest in the points of view and opinions of the children we interview. This does not necessarily imply approval of everything they do or think.

It is usually a good plan to invite children who have not reached adolescence to draw, paint or play with some of the available toys. With shy, anxious, or fearful children this is often the best way to start the interview. Conversation can then get going as the child plays or paints. Such activities help put children at ease and help establish rapport. They also enable one to observe their powers of concentration, attention span, distractibility and motor dexterity. Much can also be learned from the content of their play and of their artistic productions.

During a first interview I usually ask the child to draw her or his family. The appearance of the different family members, their order, relative sizes, positions, and even who is included and who is left out can be revealing. It can also be useful to invite the child to draw a "person" and then discuss the person (let us assume it is a boy) the child has drawn, asking questions like, "What makes him happy?" "What makes him sad?" "What makes him angry?" "What makes him laugh?" "How many friends does he have?" "Does he make friends easily?" "Do people like him?" . . . and so on. The answers to such questions can tell a lot about a child's view of the world and his or her relationship to it.

The content of children's drawings or paintings can also tell us much. Some pictures bristle with aggression: guns are firing, people are being hurled over cliffs or otherwise killed, and violence of many types is occurring. Others equally obviously convey sadness, depicting people looking unhappy or crying, feeling ill, or even being about to die. Yet others show happy scenes or illustrate the fulfillment of the artist's ambitions. Children's artistic productions should be kept with their clinical records. What they say as they draw, paint or make models should also be recorded; otherwise it is not always obvious what their productions represent. The meanings of pictures can change as they are drawn or painted; in the course of a few minutes a picture may be redefined as something quite different.

Children's drawings, paintings, and other productions must always be interpreted in the light of the overall clinical picture, taking into account all other available information. A useful source of further information on this topic is *Interpreting Children's Drawings* (DiLeo, 1983).

Adolescents may or may not wish to paint, play or draw. Much depends on their level of emotional maturity. Drawing and painting are not exclusively children's activity, and you may wish sometimes to make the point that many artists express themselves best through their own particular medium. Adolescents, especially those who feel they have some artistic talent, are sometimes glad to paint or draw on this basis. It is usually possible, as the interview with an adolescent proceeds, to judge whether it is appropriate to suggest such activities.

OBTAINING ADDITIONAL INFORMATION

Although the emphasis of this book is on the practical issue of how to interview children of different ages, it is important to remember that an interview with a child seldom stands alone. In almost all clinical situations some additional information is necessary in order to achieve the clinical objectives. Additional information is invariably needed when the aim is to understand the child or the family better. The younger the child, the more important it usually is to obtain additional information. The data that may be needed fall into four categories:

- Historical data about the child's development and previous illnesses, and descriptions of his or her current functioning.
- Information about the child's immediate family, both its history and its current functioning.
- An understanding of the extended family, in the achievement of which the construction of a genogram, or "family tree" (see Barker, 1986, p. 95–99) is helpful.
- The results of any medical, psychological and other special examinations or tests that are indicated.

Information in the first three categories is invariably helpful; that included in the fourth category may not be required in every case.

Historical and current information about the child will help make sense of many of the phenomena we observe and much of the information we gather in our interviews with children. The clinical interview is an artificial situation, quite different from most of a child's experiences. The child who does not talk in the interview may or may not talk in other situations. This is something we need to know. Many other aspects of children's behavior during interview may not be typical of what they display in other situations. Children rarely suffer epileptic seizures while we are interviewing them, and younger children may not be able to tell us that they have them. Yet it is clearly important, in understanding a child's condition, to be aware that the child suffers from epilepsy.

It is not appropriate here to go in detail into all the additional information that may be needed in the many and varied clinical situations in which we may interview children. But a comprehensive history, covering the child's conception, the pregnancy, the birth, and development up to the present time is always helpful. If some pieces of information are unavailable, our understanding of the child's case will suffer accordingly. When children of school age are being considered, it is helpful to learn of their adjustment and behavior in school and of their academic progress. If they are in paid or unpaid employment, their adjustment in these situations is also relevant. *Basic Child Psychiatry* (Barker, 1988) contains further information about how to inquire about the histories and current functioning of individual children.

Information about the family. Because children are so dependent upon their families, an understanding of how a child's family functions, and how the child interviewed fits into it is important.

Information about the extended family, that is grandparents, uncles, aunts, cousins, and even more distant relatives when they play an important part in the life of the child's family. The construction, with the help of the child or family, of a genogram or "family tree" is a good way of facilitating this.

Medical, psychological and other tests. In particular cases any one or more of a range of further tests and investigations may be required, for example, radiological investigations, including computerized axial tomography and other more recently developed methods of imaging the brain; laboratory tests of various sorts; and many types of psychological tests. The role and place of these tests are discussed further in *Basic Child Psychiatry* (Barker, 1988). The main points that need to be made here are that the interviewer should be considering, while interviewing the child, whether any further investigations or tests are necessary. If such investigations are to be carried out, you should explain to the child what is to happen and, in simple terms, why it is necessary. It is important that children know what else is to be done, if anything, following your interviews with them.

SUMMARY

Having a flexible plan assists the interviewer in moving through the introductory, information-seeking or information-giving, and concluding stages of an interview. At all times the interviewer should be sensitive to the reactions of the child and should modify the conduct of the interview accordingly.

Depending on the child's age and verbal skills, information may be obtained either in conversation or in the course of play. In many cases, a combination of the two yields best results. Children's drawings, paintings, and other artistic productions also tell us much about their personalities and emotional states.

Clinical interviews with young people rarely stand alone. What we learn during such interviews is usually only properly understood in the context of other information both about the child's current functioning at home, in school, and elsewhere, and about the family. In addition, medical, psychological, and other tests may be needed to complete a proper assessment. Interviewers should take these points into account and, when appropriate, discuss them with the young person concerned.

5

INTERVIEWING ADOLESCENTS

Adolescence is a time of change. There is a big difference between the 12- or 13-year-old who has just reached puberty and is not yet in high school and the 18-year-old who is in steady paid employment and may even be a parent. The approach that is appropriate to the first of these might be quite unsuitable for the second. So flexibility is as important to interviewing adolescents as it is to interviewing young children.

Conducting fruitful interviews with adolescents presupposes a sound knowledge of adolescent development. Without such knowledge, much that we observe in and hear from these young people will be hard to understand. Moreover many of the problems which adolescents present arise from difficulty in achieving the developmental tasks of this period. We need to be clear about what these tasks are and what are common problems for adolescents in surmounting them. Therefore I will review the main points of adolescent development before going on to a discussion of some special points about interviewing adolescents.

ADOLESCENT DEVELOPMENT—A SUMMARY

Individuals face and deal with the challenges of adolescence in many different ways. Although this period of life is widely considered a time of emotional turmoil, research studies such as those of Offer & Offer (1975), Rutter,

Graham, Chadwick, & Yule (1976), and Offer, Ostrov, & How-ard (1981) have shown that the passage through this period of life may take many courses, some smooth, others turbu-lent. Offer & Offer (1975) studied a group of male high school students in a suburb of Chicago. They identified three distinct patterns of development among this population. Twenty-three percent showed a "continuous" pattern, with a smooth, uneventful progress through adolescence to adulthood. These young men had mainly healthy, intact families, their growing independence was supported by their parents, and they had longstanding supportive peer relationships. Their images of themselves were good and they were free of psychiatric disorders.

The second group, named "surgent" by Offer & Offer (1975), made up 35 percent of the sample. These boys showed some turmoil in early adolescence, some emotional conflict, and episodes of regression. There was a certain amount of self-questioning, some anxiety about sexual matters, and a mild degree of emotional constriction. Despite these minor problems, these subjects generally developed satisfactorily, though they were involved in more conflict with their parents than the "continuous" subjects. About 36 percent of the clinical disorders in the total population studied were found in this group.

The most troubled group consisted of young people who were described as showing "tumultuous growth." They made up 21 percent of those studied. Many of them had behavior problems and mood swings, and they tended to be in conflict with their parents. About half the clinical disorders in the total population were found in this group. Another 21 percent showed a mixed pattern of development through adolescence and could not be classified into one of the above groups.

This study failed to show evidence of "adolescent turmoil" in about two-thirds of the young men studied. Similar findings were reported by Rutter et al. (1976), who studied the total population of 14- to 15-year-olds in the Isle of Wight. This island off the south coast of England consists of small towns and rural areas. While they found that disagreements between parents and their offspring about matters such as hair length and dress were fairly common, serious parent-child conflict rarely occurred except in the minority of children showing psychiatric disorders. "Inner turmoil," by which the authors meant "feelings of misery, self-depreciation and ideas of reference," was quite common, though half the sample was free of it and in some the manifestations were quite mild.

Other studies have produced similar findings which clearly indicate that the paths adolescent development may take vary greatly. In interviewing an adolescent we may or may not be facing a person in "turmoil." The reactions of young people to the challenges of adolescence are remarkably diverse.

OTHER FEATURES OF ADOLESCENT DEVELOPMENT

There are other points about adolescent development which we need to bear in mind while interviewing subjects in this period of life. The following issues are all relevant. It is often possible to inquire directly about some of them, while others need to be approached in less direct ways. Consideration of them all is necessary if our clinical work is to be effective.

1. Identity Formation

Adolescence is a time of identity formation. While the process of acquiring a sense of identity starts long before puberty, a crystallization of the sense of self occurs during this period of life. The young person comes to have rather well-established feelings of his or her self-worth, competencies, social skills and prospects in life. One of the tasks of adolescence is to prepare for life in the adult work world, for vocational choices must be made before the end of the adolescent period.

In the process of firming up their sense of identity, young people often question or even reject the views and ideas of significant adults or adults in general. This is a healthy and normal process, without which the human race would probably make little progress. The young person may be unsure of his or her identity and may be questioning ideas others might regard as self-evident. The adolescent may be anywhere along the path to a well-developed sense of identity, and may appear self-assured or unsure, confident or lacking in confidence, friendly or hostile. Attitudes and behaviors may change with a frequency that can be bewildering to the clinician trying to achieve an accurate assessment of the young person's condition. The dogmatic expression of opinions and a superficially cocksure, confident demeanor may hide deeply felt uncertainties and feelings of a lack of self-worth.

Adolescents' identities, once crystallized, do not always remain so. The identities of some adolescents are established early, only to be shattered later. Indeed, the identities of all of us are constantly being modified, at least in some degree, throughout life.

2. The Dependence-Independence Conflict

Adolescence is the period of life during which individuals normally learn to live their own lives, rather than being dependent on their families of origin. For some, the transition from dependence to independence is difficult. They usually have an urge to become independent and are subject to peer pressures fostering this. Yet they may feel inadequate and unable to meet the demands of society and their peer group, as well as self-imposed ones. An aggressively independent stance may hide underlying feelings of inadequacy.

3. Sexual Development

This is in part an aspect of identity formation, but is important enough to merit separate consideration. We need to consider both physical development and its emotional accompaniments, as they do not always go hand-in-hand.

The physical and emotional changes of puberty may occur as early as age 10 or as late as 17, though these extremes are unusual. As a general rule, to which there are exceptions, puberty comes earlier and is completed more quickly in girls than in boys. The wide differences in the time of onset of puberty and the rate of progression of the changes associated with it cause some young people to feel out of step with their peers. This is especially so for some of those to whom puberty comes late. Fears of sexual inadequacy are common during this period of life and can be anxiety-provoking.

The development of one's sexual identity and the adoption of an adult sexual role are major tasks of adolescence. The young person's progress in these tasks is often an important issue to be explored during a clinical interview.

The upsurge of sexual feelings and the development of sometimes intense relationships with the opposite sex may lead to feelings of anxiety and confusion. The desire to become involved in relationships may coexist with feelings of shyness and lack of confidence. Or the reverse may happen: adolescents may become involved in sexual activity early, perhaps in a frantic effort to fulfill their unmet needs for love, security or affiliation. This may lead to unwanted pregnancies which, whether they are aborted or carried to term, are stressful experiences.

4. Peer Group Influences

The peer group comes to assume increasing importance in the lives of most people as they pass through adolescence. This is a logical corollary to the adolescent's decreasing dependence on parents and family. Adolescent groups give support to their members in meeting the challenges of this period of life. They may be as small as two or three or membership may run to as many as 10, 20, or even more. With the support of their group, young people who are still lacking in self-confidence may be able to do things they would be reluctant to tackle on their own.

The influence of the peer group may be beneficial or harmful. Membership of a delinquent gang may have a seriously adverse effect on a young person's social behavior. On the other hand, belonging to a group of socially responsible young people can promote mature behavior and healthy personality development.

Group dynamics can have important effects on development. Many adolescent groups demand a considerable degree of conformity from their members. This may stifle members' individuality. Inability to conform to group norms may also cause members' anxiety. It may lead to their rejection from the group and this in turn may be damaging to their self-esteem.

5. The Demands of Society Versus the Individual's Level of Development

Puberty is occurring earlier than what used to be the case. In western industrialized countries the average age of the menarche is about one year earlier than it was 50 years ago. Boys are also developing earlier. Yet in these same countries young people are required to undertake longer and longer periods of study and training in order to acquire the skills needed for many jobs in industry, commerce, and the professions. Formal education and financial dependency are increasingly prolonged for those who want most of the better paid and more rewarding careers. Those who stay on at school or university tend to be more unsure of themselves and less mature; sometimes they have difficulty dealing with the conflict between the need to be independent and the necessity to remain dependent in order to stay in school. Those who choose to leave formal education in their mid or late teens often find it hard to obtain satisfying work; their prospects in the adult world may appear unpromising. This can lead to feelings of defeat and to lowered self-esteem. Some young people react with anger which they act out through antisocial or criminal behavior.

6. Family Issues

The arrival of adolescence in one of the offspring presents a challenge to the family. Adjustments in the family system are necessary. Attitudes, methods of control, and ways of relating to one's offspring which have worked well before puberty may no longer prove successful. Ideally, there should be a smooth, steady, sensitively monitored handing over of responsibility from parents to child. The parents need judge just how much responsibility and independence are right for the young person at each stage in the adolescent's developmental process. Unfortunately, not all family systems are able to respond to this challenge and make the needed changes in suitable ways. Instead of a smooth handing over of responsibility, there may develop a battle of wills between parents and offspring; or the reverse may happen, with the parents giving up control before their child is ready to shoulder the responsibilities they are relinquishing.

INTERVIEWING TECHNIQUES WITH ADOLESCENTS

The general principles and approaches set out in the first four chapters apply as much to interviewing adolescents as to interviewing younger children. The interviewer should be keenly aware of the developmental processes outlined above so as to obtain important information about the young people and make appropriate responses to their concerns. The following are some special points to keep in mind when seeing adolescents.

1. When to See the Adolescent

If there will be more than one interview with the young person and these will involve the parents or other concerned adults, it is usually best to interview the adolescent first. Esman (1988) suggests that the arrangements for the initial interview should be made directly with the adolescent, rather than through the parents. He comments that "even the unwilling, angry, defiant adolescent will often respond to the examiner's recognition that he has his own schedule of activities that deserves respect and recognition."

Adolescents who are under pressure to attend tend to be unwilling subjects. If their parents or other adults are interviewed first, they may conclude (often rightly) that unfavorable reports about them have been made before they have had a chance to state their points of view. I therefore prefer to avoid contact with the parents before seeing adolescents. Contact with the parents is better left until after the adolescent has been interviewed; or it may be made in the course of a meeting with the whole family. In the latter case the adolescent can hear what the parents are saying and is free to offer alternative points of view or versions of reality.

2. Establishing the Limits of Confidentiality

Confidentiality is a particularly important matter when adolescents are to be interviewed. The point that the interview is confidential should be emphasized early on—unless it is not entirely so, as in the case of interviews carried out at the request of courts of law. The limits of confidentiality that apply should also be described, as set out in Chapter 2.

I make it clear to the young people I interview that what they tell me will not be passed on to their parents without their permission, unless it is information so important that the parents must know—as for example when I learn that someone I am seeing is planning to commit suicide. I explain that I cannot have people leaving my office to go and kill themselves—or words to that effect. I also assure them that, in the unlikely event that I will have to tell their parents something without their permission, I will first inform them of my intention to do so.

3. The Interview as a Meeting of Persons

While all interviewers should treat those they interview with respect, the issue is perhaps of particular importance when we meet with adolescents. Many young people seen in clinical situations are in conflict with the adult world. They may have come to expect criticism and disapproval. Their behavior may be unconsciously designed to provoke such responses, which explains many of the "negative" responses we encounter when we speak with young people. I like initially to emphasize my wish to get to know the young person. I try to convey my real interest in discovering the kind of person with whom I am speaking. I encourage the young person to talk about her or his view of life, tastes in music, recreational interests, favorite pastimes and special areas of expertise.

Many young people try to shock, sometimes by using coarse language, sometimes by the content of what they say, sometimes by their behavior. Some talk of their use of street drugs or the fights they have been in, perhaps telling of how they have injured others. Unless they exceed the limits of acceptable behavior – such as performing acts of physical violence or causing damage to the furniture or the fabric of the room – I accept this sort of thing calmly and uncritically. Many young people expect judgmental responses and rejection, but these are not appropriate in clinical interviews. In due course it may be helpful to offer interpretations of the meaning of such behavior but that is a different matter. Offering interpretations is not usually appropriate in the first interview or two.

In my experience young people rarely exceed the limits I set to their behavior, once I have made these clear. The correct conduct of the interview is the best insurance against physical violence. If the limits are exceeded, some intervention, such as physically restraining the young person, may be required. Occasionally the interviewer may require assistance with this. It is well to be prepared and to know who can provide help under these circumstances, and how you will summon such help.

4. You Need Not Tell Me Anything if You Don't Want To

It is of course a truism that you cannot force those whom you are interviewing to reveal information when they don't wish to do so. Saying so can nevertheless have a salutary effect. I find it helpful, sometimes remarkably so, to make this point when the young person I am interviewing seems reluctant to answer questions or discuss issues which I believe are important. Saying, "I want to respect your privacy and if there are things you don't want to talk about today I will quite understand," or, "Sometimes people who come to see me don't feel comfortable talking about certain subjects when they first meet me and that's fine," may open up the conversation quite dramatically. Such remarks also carry the embedded message that the subject will in due course feel free to discuss the sensitive or difficult topics that are currently being avoided.

Statements such as the above are really paradoxical injunctions. Many people instinctively resist doing things when they are pressured to do them. Removal of the pressure may free them up to do precisely what they have resisted. The negativistic, resistant person may respond in such a paradoxical way when told not to reveal certain information or discuss a particular subject. For example, a delinquent teenage boy whose offenses I did not want to hear about (I knew enough about what was alleged for my purposes) insisted upon telling me what he had done as soon as I told him I didn't want to know the details of the trouble he was in!

5. What Are We Here For?

We have already seen that it is important for all concerned to be clear about the purpose of the interview. I find it helpful to discuss this in some detail with adolescents. I may ask who suggested the interview, what reason that person or those persons gave, whether the young person believes the reasons given are the true ones, whether the subject wants the interview, and if so, what he or she hopes will be achieved by it. Many related questions may arise during such a discussion, for example, whether the adolescent believes he or she actually has a problem such as to require your services, and her or his concerns about the implications of being interviewed ("Does this mean people think I'm crazy?").

6. Language and Terminology

It is always helpful to be able to speak the same language as the person you are interviewing. A knowledge of adolescents' language and the terms they use helps ensure clear communication. This does not necessarily imply using the same language. Some young people use swear words and coarse terms to try and shock interviewers and as a test of how far they are accepted as they are. Words like "fuck," "asshole," "cunt," or "motherfucker" abound in the vocabularies of some young people, especially those involved with the "street scene." My own response is to accept this sort of language without comment, unless I am genuinely unclear about what the person means. (I do not make use of such language myself and perhaps thus set a model of communication in less coarse terms.) On the other hand, it is always a good idea to ask the person you are interviewing to clarify anything you do not understand. This is one way of putting oneself in the "one-down" position which, as we saw in Chapter 3, can help promote rapport. It also provides a model of good communication.

In addition to their particular style of coarse language, young people have their own terms for the various "street" drugs and the activities associated with their supply, purchase, use and consequences. Some of the drugs young people abuse are prescription substances such as benzodiazepine tranquillizers (for example, diazepam [Valium], triazolam [Halcion], and chlordiazepoxide [Librium]), psychostimulants (amphetamines, methyphenidate), narcotic-containing medications, and barbiturates, for which they have their own names. Others are illegal drugs such as heroin ("junk"), cocaine ("blow"), lysergic acid diethylaminde ("acid") and cannabis products ("pot," "hash," "oil," and "weed"). There are many other names for these and the other drugs abused by young people and the names vary from place to place and from time to time. For example, in the province of Alberta, young people often refer to the use of "T's and R's." This is the intravenous injection of the drugs pentazocine (*T*alwin) and methylphenidate (*R*italin). This seems to be part of the prairie culture and is apparently not common elsewhere.

Blum (1984), in his *Handbook of Abusable Drugs*, lists the "street" names of many drugs and related activities. While this compilation is already somewhat out of date (as any publication dealing with the language of young people must inevitably quickly become), it is nevertheless a useful source of information. If you do not know what a "roach clip" is or what a "speedball" consists of, or what it means to "hit" someone, this and much other related information is contained in Blum's book.

LEARNING ABOUT THE YOUNG PERSON'S PEER GROUP

While it is always useful to know as much as possible about a child's peer relationships, the peer group is of particular interest during adolescence. If dependence on parents is decreasing as the young person becomes more involved with peers, as is the normal course of events, it is important to know the sort of peer group with whom the adolescent is associating. Peer group pressures can exert powerful influences in adolescents' lives.

When the process of giving up a dependent relationship with the parents is not proceeding in the normal way, it should be taken as an important piece of diagnostic information.

THE ADOLESCENT WHO WALKS OUT OF THE INTERVIEW

Occasionally angry, rebellious, or unwilling young people get up and walk out of interviews. I do not believe it is helpful to take any active steps to stop them. I usually follow them to make sure they are safe and to see where they are going. Most often it is back to the waiting room. If the young person has relatives or other adults waiting there I explain that he or she has left the interview before it was finished. I usually share my understanding of why this happened. For example, I might say that perhaps the subject being discussed was too sensitive or upsetting, or that I have the impression that the person being interviewed did not really want to be seen at this particular time. I point out that it is the young person's prerogative to decide whether to talk to me or not, and I usually offer to resume the interview after he or she has settled down or at a later date. The young person is often present while I am saying this and is thus aware of my attitude and my offer to resume the interview or conduct another one later.

If the adolescent has come for interview on his or her own, it is usually advisable to inform the parent or guardian of what has happened. This is certainly the case if there is the possibility that the young person is suicidal or might harm others, though individuals seldom come unaccompanied when they are feeling so desperate.

If the young person is seen again later, I explore the reasons behind the abrupt termination of the previous session. I make clear my wish to understand how the young person felt and I am careful to avoid any suggestion of blame. Adolescents we interview have a right to leave, though it is sometimes appropriate to discuss the pros and cons of doing so. For example, if the interview is being conducted in order that a report may be prepared for a court, the fact that the young person left before it was completed might have an adverse effect on the attitude of the court.

SUMMARY

The skillful interviewing of adolescents presupposes a sound knowledge of normal adolescent development and of how development may go awry during this period of life. "Emotional turmoil" is by no means invariably experienced by people passing through adolescence. Important issues include identity formation, resolving the "dependence-independence" conflict and becoming emancipated from dependence on parents, dealing with one's developing sexuality, acquiring a stable and helpful peer group, coming to terms with the demands of society, including the need to become economically self-supporting, and developing a new kind of relationship with one's family of origin.

Respect should always be shown for the opinions and views of the adolescent being interviewed, however much the interviewer may disagree with them. When adolescents are seen along with other family members, they should be seen either first or in company with the rest of the family. The limits of confidentiality should be established early and it is often worthwhile pointing out that the young person has a choice about what information he or she reveals during the interview. The purpose of the interview should be discussed and common ground between the interviewer and young person established. Familiarity with the language of and terminology used by young people is much to be desired. Exploration in some depth of the nature of the adolescent's peer group is also recommended.

6

MIDDLE CHILDHOOD

Middle childhood is the period from the start of formal schooling until puberty. Children in this period of life can usually tell us a lot about themselves in conversation, though their verbal skills and willingness to talk vary. Play is also prominent in their lives, and fantasy characterizes much of their thinking. We therefore have two principal channels—conversation and play—through which to communicate with children in this age group.

Flexibility and creativity are much to be desired in interviewing children in middle childhood. A quick appraisal of the type of child one is dealing with often provides clues as to how best to proceed. When a properly equipped playroom is available, some children will rush enthusiastically into it, calling it a wonderful place or exclaiming, "What a lot of toys!" They will then commence immediately to examine or play with the toys and other materials. But other children may be unmoved by such a room; they may express disinterest in the toys and deny any desire to play with the available items. Yet other children may be reluctant to separate from their families to come with you at all. The presence of severe separation anxiety in middle childhood is an important observation. We will discuss the management of the reluctant child later in this chapter.

Some children resist leaving the playroom at the end of the interview, which may indicate that you are dealing with a child who is normally deprived of attention and finds your undivided attention a novel and satisfying experience. It may also reflect the child's pleasure at meeting an accepting, approving, and uncritical adult. Yet again, it may indicate apprehension about returning to parents who are hostile and critical and who may raise objections, for example, to the fact that the child's hands are dirty.

TECHNIQUES THAT MAY BE USED IN MIDDLE CHILDHOOD

Selecting the best approach for each child is to some extent a matter of trial and error, or perhaps it is better described as a process of constantly responding to feedback. There are numerous possible approaches. The following paragraphs outline some of them. Many of these techniques are not mutually exclusive. Some may be used simultaneously or at different stages of the same interview.

(a) The "Talking Interview"

Some children prefer to communicate by talking. They tend to be those in the older years of middle childhood. Many of them are of average or higher intelligence and possess good verbal skills. Such children can be interviewed in much the same way as adolescents. They are often disinclined to play and may even be reluctant to draw or paint. Their preferences should be respected. If they are seen repeatedly, they may in due course become willing to engage in play activities.

(b) The "Play Session"

At the other end of the spectrum is the interview in which communication is almost entirely nonverbal. This may not be solely because the child lacks verbal skills, though communication must be nonverbal in the nonspeaking child; it is more often because the child prefers this channel of communication. It may also reflect nervousness. Some children who have been abused avoid talking, and this is often because they have already been "interviewed" (though in less congenial and friendly ways) by the police or child welfare authorities.

Some children simply like to play. They may belong to families in which the verbal communication of ideas is relatively little used, or they may be hyperactive children who are constantly on the go and seldom stop long enough to engage in conversation. Younger children often lack the powers of abstraction necessary to answer some of the questions which children nearer puberty are well able to handle.

As a general rule, to which there are many exceptions, younger children in the age range we are considering are inclined to use nonverbal communication while older ones tend to be verbal.

(c) Exploring the Child's Fantasy Life

The content of children's fantasy lives can tell us much about their thoughts, feelings and state of mind. Many techniques are available for doing this. These include the use of "projection tests" such as the Children's Apperception Test (or CAT), a series of somewhat ambiguous pictures which the child is asked to talk about. Such tests—and there are many others—are often administered by psychologists as a part of the process of psychological testing.

Structured tests such as the CAT will not be discussed here. Information on them is readily available in psychology textbooks and works on psychological testing. There are, however, simple ways in which the clinical interviewer can explore children's fantasy lives. We have mentioned in Chapter 4 the use of the "three wishes." This technique is particularly suited to this age range. The child is asked to imagine that if he or she could have any three wishes or, better, could wish for any three things to happen. What wishes would he or she choose?

Perhaps because this has the elements of a game and because children generally enjoy playing make-believe, most children enter into the choosing of their wishes very seriously. Some of the younger ones inquire whether the wishes will actually come true. Some older ones give responses like, "As many more wishes as I like," as one of their three.

It is remarkable how often important material emerges in the wishes. A child who has made no prior mention of family discord may come up with a wish such as, "I wish my parents wouldn't fight so much." Or one who has professed to be perfectly happy in school may say, "I wish I could always get good grades at school." Many wish for changes in their families or for different mood states. Others give indications of insecurity in their relations with peers or family and a remarkably large number of older children wish for things like, "no more nuclear war," or "no more famine or poor people in the world."

The "three wishes" question is not a standardized clinical test but it can be a valuable stimulus leading to an understanding of children's concerns. It is generally less useful in children in the early years of middle childhood than in the later ones. Younger children tend to respond to the question with requests for concrete things such as a doll, or they may simply look around the room and ask for three of the toys they see.

Asking children who they would most want to have with them on a desert island can be done in various ways. One can initially ask them to choose three people. I prefer to frame the question along the following lines: "Here's another pretend question. Imagine you were shipwrecked on a desert island. There's no-one else there but you've got plenty of food to eat and water to drink. If you could have just one person to be with you on the island – anyone in the whole world – I wonder who you would most want to have?"

Once the child has picked someone, I then go on to ask, "Now if you could have another person – the person first named and somebody else – who would you choose next?" Finally I say, "And if you could have one more – and this would be the last one you could have – who would you choose for your third person?"

While these questions do not constitute a standardized test, they can be revealing. Children close to a parent often make that parent their first choice. Others choose siblings in preference to their parents. Yet others choose entirely non-family members. These may be members of their peer group, fantasy figures, or people the child does not know firsthand, such as pop singers or television or movie stars.

There are many other ways of exploring children's fantasy lives. They can be asked what are the worst things in the whole world—and also the best things—that could happen to them. They can be asked about their ambitions in life and what they hope to do when they are grown-up. They may be asked if they ever have daydreams. If so, what do they dream about?

Day dreams

In asking any of these questions, you may need to explain what you mean or modify the questions, especially for younger children and those with limited vocabularies or delayed congitive development. For instance, not all children know what a desert island is. If I am in doubt about this, I will say, as I mention the term, "Do you know what a desert island is?" If the child does not, I will give a brief description. Similarly, some children do not know what a daydream is; if that is the case, they must be given an explanation.

Play, drawing, painting, and modelling are other channels through which children's fantasies are often expressed. We have seen, in Chapter 4, how these can all provide valuable information about children's thought content. When a child is playing with animal figures, it can be revealing to suggest pretending that his or her family members are the animals; which would be Mom, which Dad, and so on?

(d) Exploring Dream Content

I always ask children if they dream when they are asleep at night. Most say they do, though some deny remembering the content of their dreams. Sometimes those who say they do not dream or cannot remember what they dream about respond to the invitation to make up a dream, to pretend they have had one. The content of such "made-up" dreams may provide further insight into the child's fantasy life.

While the material that emerges in dreams must have relevance to the subject's state of mind, interpreting what dreams mean is not a hard science. Exploration of a child's dreams can be a useful means of gaining access to thoughts and feelings of which subjects may be unaware at the conscious level, though therapists of different theoretical persuasions may differ in their understanding of the meaning of dream material.

An exhaustive account of how dreams may be understood and interpreted is not appropriate here. However, clinicians interviewing children are well advised to take note of the content of dreams, consider their main themes, and give thought to their possible relevance to the issues the interview is designed to address. Some dreams are about lost family members or friends, others have themes of aggression which may be directed towards others or towards the person who is dreaming, yet others seem to represent the fulfillment of ambitions or fantasies. Some are happy, some are sad, some are frightening and may be dubbed nightmares. Some have themes of nurturance, others of rejection, punishment, or even death. Children suffering from nightmares may wake up emotionally distressed and require comforting by others. (Nightmares should not be confused with "night terrors" of which children do not have any subsequent recollection – see Barker, 1988, Chapter 14.) *Dreams and the Growth of Personality* (Rossi, 1985) contains much information which is of value in the understanding of dreams.

(e) Using Board Games and Other Formal Activities

Playing board games can be a useful way of making contact with children who are reluctant to say much about themselves in conversation and do not play freely with the toys and other play materials available. The games should be fairly simple and should not take too long (as games such as Monopoly do). Checkers (draughts to British readers) appeals to many children and is quite a simple game and not too time-consuming. Younger children often enjoy Snakes and Ladders. Some older ones like to play Scrabble, though this may be anathema to those with spelling difficulties. Dominoes and backgammon are other games that may sometimes be helpful in making contact and establishing rapport with children. Another possibility is chess, though this seems to have application more with adolescents than with those passing through middle childhood. If the young person is a chess player, wants to play the game and does not respond to other attempts at communication, suggesting the game may be a means of breaking the emotional ice. This applies especially to some of the more intellectual and introverted young people we see.

There are also available a number of "projective" games which are designed to give children the opportunity to express material which they may have trouble revealing in other ways. An example is *The Talking, Feeling and Doing Game* (Creative Therapeutics, 1973).

It is a good idea to have a variety of games available in a cupboard or storage space. They may include those mentioned above but many other board games are also available, with a wide variety of content and complexity. Some are concerned with relationships, other are war games with themes of aggression, still others have a variety of fantasy themes. Some have relatively serious themes, while others are "fun" games and prone to provoke laughter by having the players act things out, dress up, or make up stories. When several games are offered, the choice the child makes may in itself tell much about that child's attitudes and state of mind.

Playing board games or other formal, structured games can be more than just a means of putting the child at ease and promoting rapport. While it can certainly serve this purpose, it can also reveal much that is of clinical relevance. For example, the degree of the child's self-confidence will likely become apparent, as will his or her sense of fairness and willingness to play by the rules rather than cheat. Anger, sadness, despair, fear of failure, ability to have fun, or expectation of success may be displayed. Also likely to become evident are the child's powers of concentration and ability to understand the game and think in abstract ways. I find it often possible to get a conversation going with a child once a game is under way, even though previously the child was reluctant to talk. The game may thus become simply a backdrop to the conversation.

(f) Taking the Child out of the Office

Some children are ill at ease in professionals' offices. They may also find the environment of a formally set up playroom threatening. In that case a walk in a nearby park or in the grounds of the hospital or institution in which the child is being interviewed may prove more congenial. Other possibilities are a visit to the hospital cafeteria, the snack bar in the building in which the interviewer's office is located, or to a nearby fast-food restaurant.

Some professionals seem more inclined to venture out of their own territory than others. This is a matter of style and personal preference but it is worthwhile at least to bear these options in mind. I have on occasion used all of them, though I can only recall one trip to McDonald's in the company of a young person I was interviewing for professional purposes. I have found from time to time that leaving my territory for neutral ground and a less clinical or institutional setting has greatly facilitated the interview process.

(g) Interviewing the Child at Home or at School

Sometimes interviews with children have to be done in the home or school. The social worker investigating possible child abuse often has to visit the home and carry out interviews there. School psychologists do most of their work in school settings. Some clinicians on occasion use the school or the home as the place of choice in which to meet with a child or a family.

These settings have both advantages and disadvantages. The main advantage to interviewing people in their homes rather than in one's own office or clinic is that those being interviewed are likely to feel more at ease in familiar surroundings. The main disadvantage is that many of the conditions for a successful interview, especially the physical surroundings and availability of the play materials mentioned in Chapter 3, may not readily be met at home. Interruptions in the form of telephone calls, visitors, and a lack of privacy may make the interview process more difficult. However, much depends on the circumstances and the purpose of the interview. For example, a social worker carrying out a "home study" in order to assess whether the home is one in which it would be appropriate to place a certain child, might more naturally interview the children of the family in their usual setting.

There are some ethnic groups that are particularly inclined to feel ill at ease in clinical situations. I have found, in my practice in Canada, that this applies to many native Indian families. It can be valuable to meet with such families at least once in their home on the reserve. In many other cases, it would probably be helpful to conduct interviews both in the clinical setting and at home, but time and cost considerations may prevent this.

There are probably rather fewer advantages to interviews in school. Many children who need to be interviewed for clinical purposes have school-related problems, and therefore may not feel especially at ease there. It is advisable not to arrange interviews in the school unless that is the normal working situation of the interviewer. Perhaps the main exception to this statement concerns the situation where a clinician is making a school visit as part of the assessment or treatment of a child. The school visit may involve parents, school staff and other professionals who are concerned with the child. If the child is not part of some of the interviews or discussions that occur, a separate interview with him or her, both to balance things up and to inform the child about the discussions that have taken place, or are still going on, is usually advisable.

OTHER POINTS OF TECHNIQUE

How Focused Should the Interview Be?

The younger the child, the more "generic" the interview may have to be. In other words, it is best, at the outset, to leave younger children to define their own interests through their choice of toys and activities. The more compliant ones may seem to go along with you if you dictate how the interview should go, but this may be detrimental to obtaining the information you are seeking. For example, if a child complies with instructions to sit down and draw a picture, the result may not be as revealing as it would have been if he or she had freely chosen the means of expression. This is true especially if drawing is not a natural means of expression for the child in question.

Apart from making limits clear when this is necessary, I prefer to allow younger children to set the tone and style of the interview. This may be less necessary with older children – with them one can often discuss the aims of the interview and the work that must be done, and reach a mutually acceptable plan to achieve the goals.

Looking After Each Child's Play Materials and Productions

If the interview is intended to be one of several, it may be helpful to define what is to happen to the child's productions, be they drawings, paintings, or Plasticine models. Children often wish to show their parents what they have done or made, and they may ask to take such items home. It is important to make it clear whether this is permitted. I find it helpful, when appropriate, to ask the child to "draw a picture for me" (making it clear that it is "for me"). I may go on to say that I would like to keep it to look at again later. Some therapists, especially those carrying out long-term therapy, have a box or some lockable shelf or cupboard space for each child's toys and other materials, including artistic productions. This defines the child's work during interviews as unique, special, and valuable.

If space is limited and separate boxes or cupboard space for each child's play materials and productions cannot be provided, we should at least maintain a folder in which each child's drawings and paintings are kept.

Providing Food or Drink

I believe that most clinicians who interview children do not provide food or drink in their interview rooms. Some children, however, bring bags of chips, candies, cans of soda pop, and similar items into the room with them. My practice is to accept this as natural. But should one have available edible items such as fruit or, despite the nutritional and dental objections that might be raised, candy in some of its forms?

I am unsure of the answer to this question. I do know that some therapists, especially those conducting long-term treatment, feel it important to supply physical as well as emotional nourishment to their seriously deprived clients. Food has emotional as well as nutritional value and in the treatment of deprived children its provision can be of therapeutic value. The basic needs of many deprived and neglected children have not been met by those who have been caring for them. Food and drink are very basic requirements and by providing them for such children we can, at least in some degree, assist in the process of their recovery. How far we may need to do this will depend on the nature of our practices and the needs of particular children in them.

THE RELUCTANT CHILD

Normally developing children in the middle childhood period are sufficiently secure and free of undue anxiety to separate from their parents and be interviewed on their own. If a child is not willing to separate, this suggests that a problem exists.

The two most common causes of reluctance to leave parents are separation anxiety and a history of having previously undergone a traumatic experience or experiences in similar situations.

Separation anxiety is a normal phenomenon in younger children but by middle childhood it should occur only under conditions of stress. Its persistence in severe form is a sign of emotional insecurity. Bowlby, (1988), following Ainsworth, Blehar, Waters, & Walls, (1978), has outlined how this may develop.

Healthy development is characterized by "secure attachment." This implies that the child is confident that the parent or parental figure will be "available, responsive, and helpful," in adverse or frightening situations. As Bowlby (1988) goes on to say, securely attached individuals "feel bold in their explorations of the world and also competent in dealing with it."

Unhealthy forms of attachment behavior are "anxious resistant attachment" and "anxious avoidant attachment." The child displaying anxious resistant attachment is uncertain whether the parent will be available, responsive, or helpful when called upon. The result is anxiety upon separation from the parent, a tendency towards clinging behavior, and reluctance (because of anxiety) to explore the world. The parents of these children are usually found to have been available and helpful on some occasions but not on others. There may also have been separations of child and parent(s) and the parents may have used threats of abandonment in attempts to control the child.

Anxious avoidant attachment is seen in individuals who lack confidence that if they seek care the response will be helpful. Such young people try to live without the love and support of others. This situation seems to arise because the parents have constantly rebuffed these children when they have sought comfort or protection. In severe cases, there may have been repeated rejection and abuse or prolonged institutionalization. The longer-term results often include personality disorders and antisocial behavior.

It is children in the first category – the anxious resistant ones – who are most likely to be reluctant to separate from their parents. Understanding what may be behind their reluctance is a useful first step in dealing with them. Possible approaches include allowing the mother to accompany the child to the interview, perhaps for just part of it; showing the child where the parent(s) will be waiting; permitting the child to return to the parent(s) in the waiting room at increasing intervals of time, after the interviewer has requested the parent to respond in a suitable way; and offering reassurance that the mother (or whoever else it may be) is waiting and that the interview will end at a certain time, which can be indicated on the interviewer's watch or a wall clock if there is one in the room. Separation anxiety tends to lessen with repeated sessions, provided that the child always finds the parent(s) waiting at the end of each session.

Anxious avoidant children are not usually reluctant to separate from their parents. On the contrary, they may show singularly little concern at being seen by a strange person in an unfamiliar setting. This is itself useful diagnostic information.

The other main category of reluctant children is comprised of those who have had a frightening or otherwise emotionally traumatic experience in situations which they associate with the current clinical one. Thus children who have had adverse experiences in hospitals may anticipate that something similar will happen to them if they are to be interviewed in a hospital. Doctors, too, can be objects of fear; on hearing they are to see a doctor some children immediately ask whether they will be receiving "a needle." Such fears, arising from past experiences, must be worked through with the child as a preliminary to the interview proper.

ENDING THE INTERVIEW

It is usually wise to let children know, at the outset, how much time is available for the interview. However, this may not mean much, especially to younger children whose sense of time is as yet undeveloped. I therefore give advance notice of the end of the session, often at about ten and five minutes before it must end.

If there are toys and play materials that need to be cleaned up I initiate this process in good time. This usually ensures that the room is tidied up by the end of the session. The child's response to the request to tidy up – or to help you to do so – can be revealing. Some children readily comply, others dawdle, while yet others ignore the request or refuse to do what they are asked. Offering to help the child with the task can facilitate its accomplishment. Inviting the parents to help is another option but one to be used sparingly, if at all. It is the "difficult," behaviorally disordered children who tend to be reluctant to tidy up; their relationship with their parents may already be a mutually hostile one and bringing the parents into a situation like this may only worsen it.

I find it usually sufficient to explain that other people will soon be using the room and will want to find it as we did, that it is a rule that everyone tidies up after they have been playing, and that I will help. Very occasionally one is met with outright refusal and there is no time for further discussion or persuasion. There is then no option but to cut one's losses and tidy up oneself – or ask someone else to do so. The incident will, however, have told you much that is of clinical relevance about the child.

We have already considered the significance of the refusal of a child to leave the playroom at the end of the interview. Reluctance or refusal to tidy up may be a part of this, that is, an attempt to delay the end of the interview. When children do not want to leave, it may be necessary to state quite firmly that they can remain in the room no longer. Beyond that I have never had to do more than take the child by the hand and lead him or her back to the waiting room.

SUMMARY

Interviews with children in middle childhood require flexibility, creativity, and responsiveness to their reactions. A combination of play and talk is usually required, in addition to specific techniques to explore the child's fantasy life and the content of his or her dreams. Some children respond better to board and other formal games. These can be more than "icebreaking" devices: the child's response and approach to such games are often revealing.

Some children respond well to being taken out of the office or playroom, perhaps to a nearby park or even a fast-food restaurant. Sometimes an interview conducted at home or at the child's school may prove fruitful.

Younger children are often best left to select their own play and other activities, at least in the early stages of an interview, rather than having the interviewer impose these. Children's drawings, paintings, and other productions should be preserved; some may be worked on in a series of sessions.

Children who are reluctant to separate from their parents or other caretakers may be suffering from morbid degrees of separation anxiety, which may require special handling. Reluctance to return to the parents at the end of the interview also suggests that there may be a serious problem in the relationship between child and parents.

7

INTERVIEWING INFANTS AND YOUNG CHILDREN

> From the child of five to myself is but a step. But from the newborn baby to the child of five is an appalling distance. – L. Tolstoy (Quoted by Spengler, 1926)

As the above quotation indicates, enormous changes take place in the child during the first five years. It is a challenge to keep track of such changes and assess whether development in its many aspects is occurring normally. This is both because change takes place so rapidly, and because there are inherent difficulties in communicating with the nonspeaking and dependent infant. Very young children, and especially babies in their first year of life, cannot be interviewed in the way older children or adolescents can. If, however, we define an interview as a meeting designed to achieve the exchange of information, nonverbal as well as verbal, then it is possible to have an interview even with a baby.

The two main reasons those in the mental health and related professions are likely to be asked to see infants are:

1. To assess their developmental level.
2. To study the bonds they are developing – or not developing – with their mothers or other primary caretakers. (Throughout this chapter the term "mother" will

be used to refer to whoever is the principal caretaker of the infant concerned; in practice this is most often the natural mother, though this is not invariably so.)

DEVELOPMENTAL ASSESSMENT

Details of how motor, mental and social development normally proceeds can be found in textbooks of pediatrics or developmental psychology. The clinician working with infants and young children should be familiar with the normal course of development during this period of life and be alert for any deviations from it. Assessment of development is achieved partly by observing such things as whether the child can sit up unaided, walk, feed himself or herself, or talk in single words, short sentences or phrases, and so on – and partly by asking those caring for the child what he or she can currently accomplish in the various areas of development. Many scales are available for the assessment of infant behavior. Some of them are mentioned below.

PARENT-CHILD INTERACTION

Even from casual observation of the interactions between a mother and her baby of a few days or weeks, one can see that a great deal of communication is taking place, most of it nonverbal – though the mother may talk to the child in the course of the interaction. If communication is restricted or seems to be absent, something is amiss. Possibilities are that the child is seriously retarded or is blind or deaf. It is also possible that the parent is lacking some of the skills or motivation needed to establish communication with the infant. These problems may, in turn, be due to depression or other psychiatric difficulties in the parent. Any of these difficulties may lead to impairment of bonding between mother and child.

Interference with the process of bonding may also result when babies are seriously sick during their first weeks or months of life. If a baby is in intensive care, either because of illness or premature birth, there may be major difficulties in the establishment of emotional bonds between mother and child. Little interaction is possible if the baby is in an incubator, and in addition the baby's medical condition may cause him or her to be less responsive to the mother than a healthy, normally developing baby would be. Sometimes babies are kept in the hospital for weeks or months after their mothers are discharged, so that there may be quite limited contact between them over a long period of time.

Crying is a basic means whereby infants communicate. Lacking the capacity to speak, a baby has rather few means of communicating needs and wants to caregivers. The hungry or uncomfortable baby will cry; the contented baby will coo and respond to the presence of adults by smiling or by appearing restful and perhaps going to sleep.

Smiling is another social signal much used by babies. At first it is a reflex behavior—the "endogenous" smile—manifested by contented babies. Although not selective in the matter of who is smiled at, it serves the purpose of signaling to the caregiving adults that the baby's current needs are being met. It indicates that the infant is not hungry, cold or in discomfort. By two or three months children smile selectively at their mothers. This is the "social smile." It, too, is only manifest when the baby is content; if unmet needs such as hunger exist, the baby will cry rather than exhibit the social smile.

BONDING AND ATTACHMENT THEORY

Attachment theory was referred to in Chapter 6, but merits further consideration here. The term "bonding" refers to the process whereby individuals become emotionally attached to one another. While emotional bonds can develop at any age, the process is believed to be of critical importance during the first year of life. It is during this period in particular that the emotional bonds between children and their caretakers become established. Whether secure attachment (as described in Chapter 6) develops or whether one of the other, less functional forms of attachment (anxious resistant and anxious avoidant attachment) becomes established depends largely on what happens during this period of life.

The availability of an "attachment figure" (typically the mother) and the amount of social interaction with that person are important in facilitating the bonding process. The process does not appear to depend on the gratification of physical needs, and Harlow (1958) showed that, in monkeys, attachment can develop to a soft, cuddly dummy as well as to a live mother monkey. The notion that emotional attachment to the mother develops because she feeds the baby, while attractive at first sight, does not seem to fit the facts. Moreover, breast-fed babies do not seem to bond any differently from those who are bottle-fed.

Attachment behavior in early childhood is characterized by the attainment and maintenance of physical proximity of the child to the mother (Bowlby, 1977). During the first year of life attachment is manifested through crying, calling, stranger anxiety, and separation anxiety. The appearance and intensity of these behaviors are important indicators of how the infant is developing and of the nature and quality of the relationships existing between the child and her or his caretakers.

By about six months, the normally developing infant has learned to distinguish between familiar and unfamiliar adults and smiles selectively at the former. Then, by about eight months, signs of fear or anxiety ("stranger anxiety") appear—often shown by crying, turning away, or cringing—when unfamiliar persons are present, especially if there is no parent or other familiar person around and the infant is in an unfamiliar situation.

"Separation anxiety" usually develops soon after stranger anxiety. This is manifest upon separation from the mother (or other person to whom the child is bonded), especially in unfamiliar places or in the presence of unfamiliar people. It is a sign that the child has developed a close, secure relationship with the mother or other caretaker. In other words, bonding is well developed.

Stranger anxiety and separation anxiety normally appear early in the second half of the first year. They continue, though becoming less readily elicited, during the second year; even in later childhood they may be elicited in situations of great emotional stress. For these phenomena to appear, and for healthy emotional bonds to develop, it is necessary that the child has been cared for in a consistent, dependable way by the same person – usually the mother.

Healthy bonding depends upon the nature of the interaction that has been occurring between child and caretaker. The early months provide opportunities for us to observe the development of these phenomena. Any of the problems mentioned in the first paragraph of the section entitled "Parent-Child Interaction" may interfere with the bonding process. A main task of interviews during this period of life is to assess whether bonding is proceeding normally and, if it is not, what is standing in its way. It is necessary to make the following observations, taking into account the infant's age:

Has the "social smile" appeared?

Do the infant's reactions differ when unfamiliar, as opposed to familiar, figures are present and interacting with him or her?

Is separation anxiety present when the child is parted from the primary caretaker?

What is the general quality of the interaction between mother and child, and between other family members and the child?

Do the mother and any other caretakers of the child respond appropriately to the cues provided by the child, such as crying and smiling? Or are responses delayed, angry, off-handed, punitive, or otherwise inappropriate?

Does the child appear secure in the presence of those providing care?

OBSERVING AND INTERACTING WITH INFANTS

In addition to observing the interaction between infants and those caring for them, we can also gain useful information from direct observation of their behavior. Because separation anxiety is often quite marked, particularly during the second half of the first year, it may be best to interview infants in the presence of their mothers or other familiar figures. We can learn a great deal by observing the way children respond to others' looking or smiling at them, offers of toys, or being touched or picked up. We should pay special attention to how the infant responds when picked up and looked at straight in the eyes.

It is usually possible to play simple games with young children in the second half of the first year of life. The child might throw down or place somewhere a toy which you have given him or her, in the expectation that you will pick up the toy and allow the process to be repeated. By such means, reciprocal interaction between child and interviewer can develop. In this context it is usually possible to obtain indications of the child's emotional state, capacity to relate, alertness, motor skills, powers of concentration and attention span.

In all clinical work with children and adolescents, interviews with the parents are necessary so that a comprehensive clinical picture can be obtained. Such interviews are not the focus of this book, though they are discussed further in Chapter 12. In infancy they are of particular value, since the information that can be obtained directly from the child is relatively limited.

Discussing the psychiatric assessment of infants, Minde and Minde (1986) recommend a three-part procedure. This consists of an interview with parents or other caregivers, developmental testing of the child, and play interviews with the child.

INTERVIEWING TODDLERS

Children who have learned to walk are able to play more actively and in a wider variety of ways than infants who are not yet walking. Once children begin to talk verbal interchange also becomes possible. Therefore, there is an increasing number of ways the interviewer can interact with children as they grow older. Moreover, there is a rapid increase in both motor and verbal skills during the toddler and preschool years, that is, from roughly one year of age to about five.

Despite the increasing verbal skills of toddlers, the non-verbal components of communication with them are of paramount importance. Games such as "peek-a-boo," offering them "noisy" toys such as drums or toy xylophones that can be struck to produce sound, and telling them stories are useful approaches. It is often helpful to sit down on the floor with toddlers so as to participate more equally in their play. Some can be engaged by playing tapes of children's music. Many enjoy playing with puppets, and this is another way in which the interviewer can obtain valuable information about what is on the child's mind. Some of these techniques can also be useful in the pre-toddler stage – for example, "peek-a-boo" and the use of noisy toy percussion instruments or rattles.

Gaensbauer and Harmon (1981) describe a procedure for use in the age range 9 to 21 months. It has four phases:

(1) A free play period with mother and infant, during which the infant can play either with toys or with the mother.
(2) Approaches to the infant by a stranger and by the mother. This is designed to discover the extent to which the mother is used as a source of security.
(3) Developmental testing using the Bayley Scales of Infant Development (Bayley, 1969).
(4) A separation and reunion sequence involving the mother's departure and return three minutes later.

Gaensbauer and Harmon (1981) report differences in the responses to all four experiences in a study in which a group of "abused/neglected" children was compared with a control group of normal children.

Minde and Minde (1986) also discuss methods of examining children in the toddler age range. They recommend the use of the the Yale Developmental Schedules (Provence,

Leonard, & Naylor, 1982); they also discuss various important issues concerned with infant testing, including the vexing question of test validity. Also available for use in this age period are the Gesell Development Schedules (Knobloch & Pasamanick, 1974) and many others.

Some separation anxiety is to be expected in toddlers, especially during the second year of life. By the end of the toddler period, however, healthily developing children usually part from their parents without distress, given appropriate preparation and a suitable setting for the interview.

A properly equipped playroom is invaluable for interviews with toddlers, since communication is conducted largely through play. While children in this period of life can answer questions and often speak spontaneously, the information they give by these means is limited. Their answers are concrete and they cannot deal with abstractions. Attitudes, fears, and preoccupations are more often indicated by the content of their play.

Factual information, for example about physical abuse of a child, is easier to obtain than more abstract ideas or opinions. It is best obtained by the use of short, simple questions containing only words which are likely to be familiar to the child. Even so, young children may be reluctant to reveal such information unless they have come to know and trust the interviewer, which may take more than one interview to achieve. These issues, which are particularly critical in interviews with children who have been abused, are discussed further in Chapter 9.

PARENTAL ISSUES

Minde and Minde (1986), in their book, *Infant Psychiatry*, make some suggestions as to how the skills of the parents may be rated. Although this is somewhat peripheral to the topic of this book, the parents and their ways of handling and interacting with their infant children are important enough to merit brief mention. Minde and Minde (1986) suggest that the following parental characteristics should be rated:

General emotional and physical health.
Self-esteem.
General coping and adaptation skills.
Authoritarian versus democratic attitudes.
Willingness and/or ability to provide developmental encouragement.

These authors go on to discuss "specific parameters" of the parents' behavior that are "essential for good parenting during specific developmental stages." These are:

The ability to help the child in organizing his or her behavior.
Sensitivity and availability of the primary caretaker.
Contingent behavior. This is a matter of the caretaker's rapid response to the baby's expressed needs. Rapid response, as to the baby's crying, during the second to fourth quarters of the first year has been found to be highly correlated with the development of secure attachment of the infant to the caregiver later in life (Ainsworth et al., 1978).
Stimulation. This is a matter of the "variety, spontaneity, and richness" of the environment the caretakers provide for the child.

Also important is the assessment of parents' temperaments. These vary as widely as those of children. Some parents are more temperamentally suited than others to the care of, for example, a hyperactive child, or one prone to exhibit severe tantrums. Some are able to remain calm in the face of almost any provocation; others quickly become exasperated and react in ways which may exacerbate rather than help resolve the child's difficult behavior. The important issue of the "goodness of fit" between the temperaments of children and those of their parents is discussed more fully by Chess and Thomas (1984) in their book *Origins and Evolution of Behavior Disorders from Infancy to Early Adult Life.*

SUMMARY

Observation of infants' and toddlers' ways of interacting with their parents or other caretakers yields valuable clinical information about them. Assessment of the emotional bonds that have developed – or failed to develop – between mother and child is an important aspect of the assessment of such children.

We can learn a lot about infants and young children by observing them and interacting with them in nonverbal ways. Nonverbal behaviors such as smiling and crying are the means whereby babies communicate what older children might state verbally.

Assessing the child's level of development in its various aspects is usually an important part of the interview process. The inteviewer's impressions, based on knowledge of normal child development, may be supplemented by one or more of the various assessment schedules available.

Once children have started to speak, the observation of nonverbal communication can supplement messages obtained through conversation with them. A properly equipped playroom is an invaluable adjunct to interviewing toddlers.

Achieving an estimate of the parenting of the caregivers is also a valuable part of the examination of children, in view of babies' and young children's total dependency on their parents and the care they provide.

8

INTERVIEWING MENTALLY RETARDED CHILDREN

Geoffrey Fisher

Day after day they send my friends away.
To mansions cold and grey.
To the far side of town . . . . .
All the Madmen, David Bowie (1970)

Mentally retarded young people can be found in all situations: in our playgrounds, schools, youth organizations, courtrooms, and offices. No longer do we send them to "mansions cold and grey" on "the far side of town." For the most part, they live in our communities and we can meet them anywhere. The current emphasis on "open door" hospital policies and the community placement of retarded children means that more professionals are coming into daily contact with retarded children.

In the past, those who were unable to cope with their enviroment because of subnormal intellect were relegated to a status of "inferior citizens." Care and living arrangements ranged from closed inhuman institutions to relying on the church or charitable organizations. Often there was nothing. In ancient times it was not unusual for obviously retarded and "defective" infants to be put to death.

The idea that the handicapped have rights and needs is a very recent development. The concept of "normalization" considers each retarded person as an individual. It does not mean "training" retarded children, for example by behavioral methods, to be acceptable to society's norms. Instead it means accepting the child with his or her limitations, setting realistic expectations and meeting his or her needs in the least restrictive way.

To be considered retarded, a person must be retarded in terms of both intellectual ability and adaptive functioning. The major point is that a retarded person is handicapped in adapting to the norms of his or her social group. It does not imply that mental retardation is a single "disease entity." Any clinical evaluation therefore must be comprehensive and always requires an interview of one sort or another.

Interviewing a retarded child demands skill, careful observation, and above all patience. Some of us are intuitively good at interviewing children, only to find ourselves stumbling with a retarded child. Others have little or no difficulty, but attention to certain factors can improve the quality and effectiveness of anyone's interviews.

This chapter will outline what mental retardation is (and is not), along with a brief review of some of the common and special problems encountered. Strategies for interviews will then be presented.

THE NATURE OF MENTAL RETARDATION

Mental retardation is a lifelong condition with multiple and often interacting causes that make life more difficult and stressful than it is for those of normal intellect. Even though there are no cures for mental retardation, we can, with appropriate management, dramatically improve the quality of life for retarded children.

The primary handicap is diminished intellectual capacity. Using standardized tests the figure of 100 is taken as a measure of average intelligence. Anyone with a score on intelligence tests two standard deviations below this, that is with an intelligence quotient (I.Q.) of 70 or less may be considered mentally retarded. Although convenient for comparing retarded individuals with the general population the measured intellectual level gives limited indication of overall social adjustment.

The causes of mental retardation are legion. They include genetic and chromosomal abnormalities, prenatal infections, perinatal injuries and illnesses, and enviromental factors. A general rule of thumb is that the more severe the retardation, the more likely it is due to organic factors.

SPECIAL FEATURES OF MENTAL RETARDATION

Physical handicaps are more common in the severely retarded. There may be various paralyses, difficulties in controlling limb movements and coordination, deafness, blindness, and speech problems. They complicate the primary handicap and frequently are the limiting and deciding factors of social adjustment. For example, a child may be capable of basic understanding of his or her environment, yet may need hospital care because of added cerebral palsy.

Retarded individuals have special problems with communication. The greater the retardation, the worse their language and speech abilities tend to be. In some cases, additional physical problems, such as cerebral palsy or abnormalies of the palate, can cause the persons' language skills to appear worse than they really are. The person may be able to communicate quite adequately using drawing or special communication equipment such as a customized computer system. The profoundly retarded lack verbal language but may be able to indicate their needs through emotional outbursts or primitive vocalizations. The severely retarded may be able use vocalizations, single words, and sometimes two- or three-word phrases. The moderately retarded are usually capable of adequate though elementary communication using simple sentences. They can use words to give uncomplicated descriptions of emotions, such as fear and sadness. Mildly retarded children have speech that is simple in grammar and syntax and "concrete" in style. Some retarded children suffer from specific language disabilities, in addition to the effects of intelligence on language. These need to be distinguished as specific treatments may help.

Retarded children are more vulnerable to emotional, psychological, and psychiatric problems than those of normal intelligence. Rutter (1975) estimated that some 30 to 40 percent of retarded children were rated as disturbed by their parents, about three times more than an equivalent nonretarded group. The prevalence of psychiatric disturbance in the retarded is uncertain, but some 50 percent probably have some degree of emotional or psychiatric problem. The majority of these disturbances are behavioral, though it must be remembered that behavioral disturbance may only be a symptom of an underlying mental disorder such as depression or an adjustment reaction.

Psychotic illnesses are known occur in retarded children, though the exact prevalence is unknown. In the more severely retarded, it is difficult to diagnose such illnesses; this is especially so in the profoundly retarded. Accurate psychiatric diagnosis depends, in part, on analyzing talk and thought processes. This is virtually impossible with severe degrees of retardation. Sometimes a change in behavior may be the only sign. In these cases, accurate and highly tuned observational skills are essential. Also, someone who knows the child and his or her nature and habits should be available to provide information before or at the interview. Nearly all severely and profoundly retarded children show evidence of organic brain syndromes, and this increases their susceptibility to psychiatric illness.

Making a diagnosis of depression presents difficulty in the retarded. Depression is usually diagnosed when people are able to tell us of their suffering and misery. A severely retarded person cannot do so. The only indicators may be gradual withdrawal, loss of appetite and sometimes outbursts of temper. All too often severe depressions have been left untreated because the withdrawal and temper has been labeled as "bad attitude." Retarded children and adults are known to cope poorly with change and often respond to this with severe behavioral outbursts. These may represent episodes of depression and require treatment with antidepressants rather than devising punitive measures for the behavior.

Diagnosis is no easier with the less retarded. Their level of language and speech may enable them to cope with everyday tasks. Yet their intellect and vocabulary may be insufficient to convey fine distinctions of mood or describe hallucinatory and delusional experiences.

Emotional disorders are most clearly seen in moderately retarded children. They have only limited coping skills; a fight with a sibling, a move of house, the removal of a toy, or a period of "time-out" in a bedroom as a consequence can be very traumatic. A stressor that may be trivial to a normal child may be catastrophic to a retarded one.

One added handicap to which retarded children are especially susceptible is the effect of stigma. In this respect they are similar to the physically handicapped. The sequelae can be wide-ranging and serious. Defects in self-esteem can be profound and may go unrecognized. The mildly retarded are aware of their handicap and usually look normal. This may expose them to expectations which they may be unable to meet. These children are also vulnerable to anxiety and depression. Sometimes chronic frustration and self-doubt may lead mildly retarded adolescent boys into conflict with the law, and some girls into prostitution.

Mental retardation is not a unitary concept. It ranges from mild to profound and has added layers of secondary handicaps of varying degrees and nature. It is these secondary handicaps, to some extent, that dictate the quality of a retarded child's life and whether the child needs special care.

ATTITUDES TO THE MENTALLY RETARDED

Attitudes to the retarded vary. They range from fear to indifference and, in some rare cases, open hostility. A developing child's experience of the world depends on the responses of those around him or her. Apprehensions about the retarded are common. Unwittingly our society may be responsible for making it more difficult for the retarded to adapt socially. Professionals are not immune either. Alford and Locke (1984) showed that a label of "mental retardation" adversely biased the clinical judgment of a group of doctoral level psychologists when assessing therapy transcripts. Menolasco, Gilson, and Levitas (1986) comment on how such attitudes may affect transference and countertransference issues in the management of the retarded in the community.

On occasion parents of retarded children "shop around" for suitable caregivers. Anderson (1971) considers this behavior as "a learned response to unsatisfactory contacts with professional people regarding their child." We have come a long way since the days of referring to the retarded as "idiots," "imbeciles" and "morons," but it is clear we still have far to go.

INTERVIEWING RETARDED CHILDREN

In view of the almost infinite variations in presentation, setting, and attitudes, how do we go about planning interview strategies?

Chapter 3 discusses the physical surroundings for interviews with children. The general principles outlined there apply here but certain minor modifications are necessary. The room should be large enough to comfortably accommodate a wheelchair. Retarded children often cannot draw, paint, or play games at regular tables either because of coordination difficulties or because the wheelchair will not fit under the table. A bench of suitable height to accommodate a wheelchair is helpful. However, if this is not available, tables, similar to those used in hospitals that can be wheeled over a bed may be used. Sloping wooden easels resting on the child's knee while he or she sits in a wheelchair may serve as alternatives. A large foam filled mat should be available so that a child may lie on the floor to draw or play with toys.

Crayons, pencils and paint brushes should be of appropriate size and thickness for children with muscle and coordination problems to grasp easily. Large toys such as dollhouses should not be permanently fixed to tables; they may need to be placed on the floor so that multiply handicapped children can use them.

The "playroom" is not always the place to interview retarded children. Mildly retarded adolescents can comfortably be interviewed in the office, though books and drawing materials should be available.

PLANNING THE INTERVIEW

The primary guiding principle is that any interview should be comprehensive and contextually related to the reason why the interview is needed. Retarded children may need to be interviewed as part of an assessment for residential, day or school placement, or questioned by the police about their alleged participation in some crime. Such interviews will be very different from those used by psychiatrists to assess the presence or absence of mental illness in children.

Before the interview, it is important to obtain certain background information regarding the child's usual habits and abilities. The families of retarded children usually have available much of the information needed and are willing to allow this to be used. An initial telephone call to the parents or guardian should be followed up with a polite letter asking for the information required or requesting the appropriate consent to obtain this before the appointment date. Enclosing a "family information questionnaire" with the letter can be helpful. This covers details of parental occupation and other children in the family. The use of self-addressed, stamped envelopes improves compliance.

Interviewers can obtain useful information from schools and special attendence centers about the child's academic and social abilities. Copies of school reports covering a two- or three-year period may be needed. It is important also to request that the teaching or care staff provide a summary of the child "as a person." This should not be a technical document, but an overview of the child's strengths and weaknesses, likes and dislikes, the games he or she may enjoy and so forth.

In almost all cases a retarded child has previously undergone psychological testing. The results should be reviewed. We should record the measured intelligence plus any added handicaps such as speech or language difficulties. If the testing person observed any special problems in managing the interview or techniques that were sucessful in bypassing handicaps, he or she should keep careful note of them.

With severe degrees of retardation, the diagnosis is not usually in doubt, but errors can occur with the less severely retarded. If there is any doubt about the diagnosis, then we should examine closely past testing and assessment. In some cases, past medical records such as birth records, and attendances at developmental assessments can provide clarification, in addition to psychological testing.

Thus before the child is seen, the interviewer should have a comprehensive knowledge of the child's functioning in various areas. There are so many pitfalls in the assessment of a retarded child that we should take into account all information that can be obtained during the process.

THE INTERVIEW DAY

When arrangements are being made for the interview, it is important that the child's caretakers – most often the parents – attend as well. If the family has more than one parent, both parents should be invited. Much information on family functioning may be lost if they do not both attend. This may mean having to schedule the interview to avoid work hours. Sometimes, if the collected information suggests a particularly complex problem, such as a possible mental illness or difficult placement issues, the parents or guardians may need to be interviewed on a separate occasion before the child is seen. Occasionally the background information will suggest some degree of family dysfunction; in such cases one should consider seeing the whole family living in the home prior to seeing the child alone.

As retarded children are sometimes upset by changes in routine, parents should be informed before the interview to keep the day of the interview as "routine" as possible. If the child usually has a snack in the morning or afternoon, the parents should be allowed to bring this to the interview. If possible the child should be told of "the visit with mommy and daddy" to "talk" or "play games" in a matter-of-fact manner. Strenuous play or exercise should be avoided before the interview as many retarded children easily become excited and take time to calm down. They may also feel nervous, particularly if they are moderately to mildly retarded and associate "visits" with "tests." Engaging very nervous children in a favorite activity or treat just prior to the interview may have a calming effect. Allowing them to bring to the interview a comforting soft or favorite toy can be helpful. These strategies should be outlined to the family in the letter of introduction.

THE INTERVIEW

The waiting area for the interview should be furnished with toys and activities which the child should be allowed to explore. This may help settle an otherwise nervous child. Allowing about ten to fifteen minutes of waiting is usually no problem. But as waiting periods extend, children with attentional or behavioral difficulties may become unsettled and apprehensive. Parents may also be nervous, especially if much depends on the results of the assessment. Many retarded children, just like their normal peers, are sensitive and reactive to their parent's emotions. Excessively long waiting time only serves to compound difficulties; thus being punctual is not only a matter of courtesy but also necessary.

The family should be greeted with introductions and handshakes, and then escorted to the interview room. These preliminaries are important and frequently set the tone of the interview. It is important to make initial observations and impressions at this point. The child may be oblivious to the interviewer or may seem to be excessively shy or to fail to respond to parental directions. Sometimes one parent may seem eager to get on with things and the other may appear disinterested or reserved.

It is particularly important with retarded children to begin the interview with all present. This allows the child to settle with those familiar to him or her. The first few minutes are very important. The interviewer's task is to put the family at ease and orientate them to the organization of the interview. The reasons why the child needs to be interviewed should already be clear, but they must be clarified with parents at this point. There may be misunderstandings. Important initial and practical information can be acquired at this time, such as observing physical handicaps and assessing the child's speech. It is useful to ask questions of parents about specific handicaps or problems and any "tricks" they know to get around these. It is also the time to start developing rapport with the child in the presence of his or her parents.

Many interviewers spend some time getting to know the family and hearing their story. This may take 30 minutes to an hour or even longer. This may be quite an acceptable procedure for children of normal intellect, but retarded children often have difficulties with attention span and restlessness. The introductory and clarification part of the interview with retarded children should therefore be kept short. I recommend no longer than 15 minutes. It is better to get on quickly with the individual interview; if serious issues do arise, arrangements can always be made to see the parents or guardians at a later date.

With children of normal intelligence, it is often possible to complete an interview in a single session of 45 minutes or so. This may not be possible with retarded children. Not only do they tire easily, but sometimes added physical handicaps and communication difficulties make the interview more time consuming. Retarded children are slower in their physical abilities and it may take time, for example, to set up a painting activity for a moderately retarded child in a wheelchair. Various degrees of cerebral palsy or other difficulties with coordination may prolong a simple sand tray game. Poor speech and language skills may extend information-gathering and instructions. Parents should be informed of these potential problems at the interview orientation and told that more than one interview will usually be necessary. I have found that appropriate assessment of a retarded child usually takes three separate interviews of between 30 and 45 minutes each.

INTERVIEW STRATEGIES

Interviewing retarded children follows essentially the same format as that for children with normal intelligence. However, modifications are necessary to meet the needs created by physical and communication limitations. For the purpose of discussion, the interview can be divided into three stages: introduction, observation, and exploration. In practice, these stages merge. Rigid interview schedules are not recommended, though basic data relevant to each stage must be obtained. The three stages should help the interviewer organize the procedure in his or her mind.

The introductory stage involves establishing and building rapport and assessing communication skills. If the child is in the playroom, he or she should be allowed to explore and comment upon the toys. We can ask basic questions at this point about the toys, what the child may like to play with, or whether he or she has been to this hospital before. Such neutral questioning enables the examiner to assess the child's speech and language skills. It is important to differentiate between language difficulties and other disorders of communication. Speaking to the child in a language too simple or childlike may be perceived as insulting; conversely using too complex and sophisticated language may result in misunderstanding. Many mildly and moderately retarded children are aware that they do not understand but are fearful to admit this. Approximate language abilities can be inferred from the child's measured intelligence and can serve as a rough guide.

If the child is capable of understanding, we should give the child reasons for interviewing him or her. Mildly retarded children may be apprehensive and expect to be tested; if so, we should reassure them when no test is needed. If testing is indeed one of the reasons for interviewing the child we should reframe the information in terms of games or activities. The child should be allowed to explore various activities offered in the room. Emotionally charged topics should be avoided at this stage, though general questioning about family members is usually acceptable.

With profoundly or severely retarded children, it will be clear very quickly that speech abilities are rudimentary or practically absent. This does not mean that one cannot communicate at least at some level. Sitting directly in front of the child and smiling may elicit a response. So may gently stroking the child's hand or face with your hand or a piece of fur. Singing a simple melody or using tape-recorded children's songs while touching the child can be effective. Sometimes we can find out whether the child can respond to something by taking the child to a window or playing with puppets.

Body language is very important with nonverbal children. You should seat yourself in such a way that your eyes are at the same level as the child's. If this means that you have to sit on the floor then you should do so. Towering above a nonverbal, possibly fearful child can provoke anxiety. The interviewer should neither get too close too quickly nor sit on the other side of the room or table. If you need to touch the child, you should do it slowly and without surprising the child.

The use of hand movements and facial expressions can facilitate communication, as can modeling or "following" the child's movements. I have found that nonverbal retarded youngsters are particularly sensitive to and aware of these nonverbal means of communication.

Some mildly retarded deaf children can use sign language.

If you can sign also, then by all means do so. Most of us are unable to sign, and sometimes the child may be too handicapped to have learned the necessary skills. In these cases, communication can still be established by using drawings or modeling instructions and activities for the child to follow.

Blind retarded children are especially prone to fear and anxiety. If they are capable of understanding, then all directions and activities must be slowly and carefully explained. For example, it is unwise to touch a blind child without asking permission first. If the child is blind and severely or profoundly retarded, then touch and sound are the only methods of establishing contact. The use of soft fabrics and quiet background music can be helpful. A useful technique is to ask the parents to demonstrate how they approach and touch their child, and then to ask them to guide your hand in the same manner. Sometimes it is valuable to have a parent present during the interview with a child with multiple special sensory handicaps.

Some interviewers find it difficult to believe that a profoundly retarded child is capable of communicating, but it is best to assume that some communication is possible rather than that the child is completely cut off from his or her surroundings. On the whole, we tend to underestimate the abilities of our retarded patients. Occasionally all of the first interview may be spent trying to establish a method of communication. In such cases it is not a waste of time and may yield much valuable information. The development of rapport cannot be separated from the process of establishing communication, as is discussed in Chapter 3.

Throughout the establishment of communication and rapport, valuable observations will have been made. Already you will have formed an impression of the child's attention span, level of distractibility, temperament, communication abilities, and motor and coordination skills. It is useful to have in mind a "checklist" of behaviors to be noted. At some point in the interview, when the child is occupied on a task, it is useful to review this list. Particular behaviors to be noted include the child's response to emotionally charged subjects.

Retarded children can be just as upset or sensitive as their "normal" peers. Changes in behavior or outbursts of temper may be seen under such circumstances. Similar reactions may be observed if a task or game is replaced by a different one. The child's reaction to activities such as drawing or writing his or her name may reveal frustration. Some children express frustration while performing a task due to fear of failure; others fail to complete an activity because of motor coordination problems; and still others perform well below their expected ability because they are conditioned to failure and are expert in their avoidance of tasks. I have observed that some children "play" at appearing helpless, when in fact they are capable of far more than they or their families believe. This is also a reason why the results of intellectual testing should be treated with caution until the child has been personally assessed. It is not unknown for a past measurement of low intelligence to become a self-fulfilling prophecy.

It is sometimes difficult to determine the exact nature of observed autistic or "autistic-like" behaviors which include gaze avoidance, an aloof, disinterested attitude, "flapping" of the arms and hands, swirling round and round, and licking and mouthing objects. These "autistic" features can be seen in varying degrees in non-autistic retarded children. To complicate matters, 70 percent of autistic children have a measured intelligence quotient of less than 70. When confronted with such puzzles, the best approach is simply to record the behavior without interpretation. The use of videotape recordings in such situations can be helpful. After the interview, the observations can be placed in the context of the developmental and medical history. Interviewing autistic children is discussed further in Chapter 11.

When rapport, communication, and initial observations have been achieved, you should have a clear idea of the child's strengths, weaknesses, and typical responses. Achieving this may have taken one or two interviews. You may now explore specific areas, including emotionally sensitive issues. Precisely what is to be explored will depend on the reasons for the interview. A psychiatrist may need to assess the presence or absence of mental illness or sequelae of abuse. A social worker or teacher may need to assess the child's strengths and weaknesses for future living or school arrangements. As before, the techniques of exploration previously outlined in Chapters 1, 3, 5, and 6 can be followed, again with modification.

With verbal children, the balance between direct and non direct questions is important. The majority of children seen are verbal and only mildly retarded. They tend to present themselves as favorably as possible. Often they seek to please the examiner with "appropriate" answers to questions, especially when sensitive issues are being explored or when they feel under pressure. Shaw and Budd (1982), in a study of mentally retarded adults, found that "naysaying" occurred more frequently when prohibited subjects were discussed, and the subjects responded positively when desirable behaviors were raised. Sigelman, Budd, Spanhel, & Schoenrock (1981a) titled a paper on acquiescence in interviews with retarded persons: "When in Doubt, Say Yes," and later showed that questions demanding "yes" or "no" responses result in invalid information (Sigelman, Budd, Spanhel, & Schoenrock, 1981b). The same paper notes that using carefully worded "either/or" questions influence the responses less than "yes/no" questions. I have frequently observed this with retarded adolescents, and it is common in children of all degrees of intellect. The use of multiple-choice questions, along with pictures, also serves to increase the validity of answers (Sigelman, Budd, Winer, Schoenrock, & Martin, 1982).

When probing for information, we should pay special attention to balancing "prompting" and "open-ended questions." All children require prompting and encouragement from time to time. Open-ended exploratory questions become progressively less useful with increasing retardation and younger age. Sigelman et al. (1982) comment that the retarded often find open-ended questions unanswerable. Retarded children need more prompting than their normal peers. Bearing in mind the tendency for retarded persons to acquiesce in response to certain questions we must avoid the overuse of prompting. If you find yourself relying heavily on prompting, you may do better to abandon questioning altogether and to use nonverbal techniques, such as play in the dollhouse or sand tray. This is especially important in cases of alleged sexual or physical abuse of a retarded child. False accusations or inability to validate any allegations can be equally disastrous.

Problems arise with the recall of information. Dent and Stephenson (1979) found that with children of normal intelligence unprompted recall of an incident was most accurate. However, in view of the fact that the retarded do not respond well to openended questions some degree of prompting is necessary. Dent (1986) experimented with different techniques of questioning mentally retarded children with an intelligence quotient range of 50 to 70. Free recall, general questions and specific questions were asked the group of children about an event staged in their classroom. She found that asking general questions (midway between free recall and specific questions) produced optimal recall. The implications for mentally retarded witnesses are significant. The asking of general questions during the course of a routine office assessment can be very helpful. However, a mentally retarded youngster charged with a crime or appearing as a witness or victim of abuse may be anxious when discussing emotionally laden topics. Frequently, no clarification can be obtained in either direction. Under some circumstances, the use of videotaped interviews conducted in less stressful enviroments is admissible in court or may be used in child protection investigations.

Throughout the interview, careful use of reinforcement is required. Positive verbal comments are generally used, but overuse of reinforcement can bias answers as much as poorly worded questions. With severely retarded children, nonverbal reinforcements, such as stroking or gently squeezing the child's hand, may be used. On occasion candies can be helpful.

As we can see, interviews with retarded children can vary a great deal and rely heavily on establishing communication and observing behaviors and reactions. With severe degrees of retardation, these may be all we have to go on. We tend to assume that a "good" interview depends on eliciting information via questioning. This is incorrect.

Other erroneous assumptions are that the problems of retarded children are unique, and that mental retardation is "a separate disease entity" requiring unique solutions. These, too, are incorrect.

Retarded children differ only in degree from their "normal" peers. The interviews in reality are not that different in format or content from those with nonretarded children. Knowledge of the children's limitations, comprehensive and planned information-gathering and history-taking, careful observation, and above all, patience are the ingredients for effective and enjoyable interviews.

SUMMARY

Knowledge and understanding of the specific handicaps that affect retarded children are essential for good interviewing. These handicaps include physical problems, communication difficulties, and emotional problems. Careful and planned collection of background information is necessary. Minor modifications are required to the interview room.

Establishing rapport is important, as is attention to both verbal and nonverbal cues. The suitable phrasing of questions is essential if good information is to be obtained. Aside from careful observation of the child's behavior, patience is perhaps needed above all else.

9

THE CHILD WHO MAY HAVE BEEN ABUSED

The considerable prevalence of child abuse in its various forms – physical, sexual, and emotional – has increasingly been recognized during the last few decades (Barker, 1988, Chapter 18). Any clinician engaged in interviewing children is liable to come upon evidence of past or current abuse. Therefore whether or not we are practicing primarily in the field of child abuse, we must be alert to these possibilities and know how to proceed when evidence of abuse emerges.

It is not possible in this volume to deal comprehensively with the examination and assessment of abused children. This has become a clinical speciality in its own right, and in many centers there are agencies, teams and clinicians who have developed special expertise in this field of practice. My aim here is to give the clinician who is not a specialist in this area guidelines on how to proceed when evidence emerges that abuse may have occurred. Further information may be obtained from the many publications now available on child abuse. Useful sources of information are *The Battered Child* (4th edition) (Helfer & Kempe, 1987), *The Psychologically Battered Child* (Garbarino, Guttman, & Seeley, 1986), *Handbook on Sexual Abuse of Children* (Walker, 1988), and *Interviewing the Sexually Abused Child* (Jones & McQuiston, 1988).

The growing awareness of the various forms of child abuse

makes it increasingly likely that relatives and referring professionals will bring up the possibility of abuse when we interview children. While the general principles that apply to these interviews are the same as those that apply in other cases, some special points should be borne in mind.

PRELIMINARIES

If abuse is suspected or evidence of it comes to light, it is especially important to be clear about for whom the interview is being conducted. We should carefully consider the question of consent. If abuse by someone outside the immediate family circle is suspected, issues of consent seldom present problems, because the parents or guardians are probably outraged or angry about what they suspect may have happened, and are eager to have the matter investigated and to seek appropriate help. If the question of intrafamilial abuse arises, however, the situation may be different. If the interview has been requested by a child protection agency or by the police or a court, it is generally wise to ensure that you have received a written request to carry it out and that the person or agency making the request has the legal status to authorize the interview.

Sometimes it is unclear, at the outset, whether suspected abuse was extrafamilial or intrafamilial. Abuse may emerge in the course of an interview that was requested for other reasons, for example, deteriorating school performance, unexplained anxiety or other neurotic symptoms, disturbed behavior such as running away, or physical problems ranging from fractures or other injuries to urinary or genital tract infections. In most jurisdictions, it is then incumbent on the interviewer to report his or her suspicions to the appropriate authorities, usually the statutory child welfare agency or the police. Further investigation is then planned in cooperation with the authority concerned and may or may not involve the clinician who initially saw the child.

The recommendations made earlier (Chapter 3) about the optimal setting for interviews with children apply equally to interviews with those who may have been abused. If sexual abuse is suspected it may also be advisable to have available (though not initially in view) a set of "anatomically correct" dolls. The use of these dolls is discussed below, in the section on sexual abuse.

When issues of child abuse arise, it is important to have on hand someone with the skills and experience needed to handle these often difficult cases. This work should not be undertaken by the unsupervised novice. Some clinicians are more comfortable dealing with these cases than others. Dealing with sexual abuse can be particularly emotionally taxing; those who are uncomfortable in this area of clinical practice may be better of seeking consultation and support from others with experience in the area, when they find themselves dealing with such cases. In addition, the interviews may lead to the necessity of giving evidence in court – a point to keep in mind from the start.

Obtaining as much background information as possible, before the interview, is essential in cases of suspected abuse. This may alert the interviewer to various possible pitfalls. Particularly difficult are those cases in which a parent is suspected of being the abuser. It is important to avoid interviewing such children in the presence of parent or parents.

There are advantages to having more than one interviewer present. This may increase the amount of information that is acquired; one person may concentrate on talking to the child and asking the appropriate questions, while the other observes nonverbal behavior and perhaps takes notes on the process and content of the interview. An alternative is to have the observer, or more than one of them, behind a one-way observation screen. In that case, the child should be introduced to the observer(s) before the interview starts and should be shown the one-way screen and told how it works. Many children seem to forget quite quickly that they are being observed.

It is essential to keep a good record of these interviews. What the child says, the context in which things are said, and the nonverbal behavior that accompanies statements and responses to questions should all be recorded. A second person in the room or behind a one-way screen can be of great assistance in achieving this. Another possibility is to record this information on videotape; however, suitable equipment and technical assistance may not be available, and the fact that the interview is being recorded on tape may inhibit the child and prevent the disclosure of sensitive information. The presence of an additional person in the room may have a similarly inhibiting effect; therefore, observation from behind a one-way screen may be preferable.

In many clinical situations, there may be no suitably skilled colleague available to observe the interview. Video recording equipment or the technical help necessary to obtain a good quality recording may also be unavailable. Therefore many interviews of possibly abused children are likely to be carried out by clinicians acting on their own. In such cases, the importance of immediately preparing or dictating a detailed report after the interview cannot be overstressed. While I do not like to make written notes while interviewing, I often do so in these cases.

THE INTERVIEW ITSELF

Children of any age may be victims of abuse. The conduct of the interview will depend in part on the age of the child, and also on whether the child is aware of its purpose. Adolescents often are aware of the purpose; indeed, interviews with them frequently follow their disclosure of the abuse, or their allegations that it has occurred. This sometimes applies also to those in middle childhood, in the age range of 7 to 11. If the interviewer talks or asks interminably about unrelated matters, the young person may wonder what is happening and perhaps begin to question the competence of the interviewer. An already anxious and apprehensive subject may become increasingly tense while waiting, with anticipation, for the subject to come up. In such cases, it is often best to come quite quickly to the point.

If the child is unaware that abuse is suspected or that this is a reason for the interview, a slower, gentler approach is usually in order. Time used to establish rapport is well spent. It is generally unwise to proceed to questions concerning possible abuse until rapport is well developed and the child has come to trust the interviewer. Since this situation may not be achieved in the first interview, it may take several interviews to elicit the information sought.

When interviewing children who may have been abused, it is advisable to be careful in making physical contact. Even sudden movements by the interviewer may cause the child to wince or put his or her hands up in a defensive gesture. If you consider it helpful to make physical contact during play activities or games, you should first obtain the child's permission.

Rigid interview schedules are not desirable, but it is a good idea to have questions ready and to ask them in a clear and matter-of-fact, but sensitive way. Hesitant or fumbling questioning tends to damage rapport. If children sense that you are in some way ill at ease in asking, for example, about behaviors which constitute sexual abuse, they are likely to become ill at ease themselves.

THE PROS AND CONS
OF LEADING QUESTIONS

Questions regarding possible acts of abuse should generally be open-ended and as nonspecific as possible. "Can you tell me what happened?" is better than "Did he hit you?" "Has anyone ever done anything to you that you felt uncomfortable about?" is better than "Has anyone ever touched you down below?" (or "in your private parts?"). Once information is disclosed the questions can become more specific, but it is always important not to put ideas into the child's mind. To facilitate this process it is helpful to have a prepared list of questions ready in your mind.

If open-ended and nonspecific questions yield no response, it may be necessary to ask specifically about acts of abuse, but information so obtained does not have the same value, either clinically or in the course of legal proceedings, as that which is revealed without the use of such questions.

PHYSICAL ABUSE

As with clinical interviews generally, so also in cases of suspected physical abuse: the younger the child, the more we must rely on nonverbal information. A careful physical examination is essential in every case. This often needs to be supplemented by X-rays and sometimes by other special investigations, as when injury to the kidneys, eyes, brain or other organs is suspected. In this book, however, I will not deal with the physical assessment of these children, which should be carried out by a physician experienced in this work. Instead, I will focus on the process of interviewing the child. It is important to read carefully any previous medical, X-ray, laboratory or other reports relating to the child before carrying out the interview.

When abuse has occurred, there may be telltale signs in the interaction between the abusing person and the child. This is frequently the case when the abuser is a parent, stepparent or common-law partner of a parent. The child may appear fearful in the parent's presence and may cry when the parent approaches. Abnormalities in the interaction between parent(s) and child may suggest that there are abnormalities of attachment and bonding. There may be the phenomenon of "anxious–resistant attachment" to the parent, but more common is the "anxious-avoidant" infant (both are described in Chapter 6). These infants do not seek close contact when reunited to their mothers after a period of separation. Even in high-stress situations, they appear happier away from their mothers.

Another behavior which may be seen in abused children, even quite young ones, is "reversed caring," also known as "role reversal." The child is constantly seeking to look after the parent, for example, offering the mother a cigarette, lighting it, hastening to fetch things the parent wants, and so on.

With young children, especially those with little in the way of verbal language, the content of play can be revealing. If such children are invited to play with family figures, for example in a dollhouse, they will often play out the kind of things that go on in their homes. For instance, the "child" figures may be shouted at, threatened or hit. An atmosphere of violence may characterize the interaction between children and dolls. The doll children may be crying, or pleading not to be hurt. There may be much talk about the children being "bad" or naughty and little in the way of affirmation or positive statements.

Similar material may emerge in abused children's play with animals or non-family figures (for example soldiers); it may be apparent, too, in their drawings and paintings. In the course of play or other activities, the interviewer may join the child and invite him or her to expand on what is being played out. For example, if a "child" figure is being beaten, the interviewer might ask, "I wonder how that feels for him?" Or again, "I wonder what he (or she) has done to be punished like that?" Such questions may serve to "externalize" the problem, which may make it easier for the child to talk about it. Another response that may prove fruitful is to ask, "Has anything like that ever happened to you?" Such relatively open-ended questions may lead to the disclosure of important information. More specific questions can follow once the child has stated clearly that he or she has, for example, been subject to physical violence. These may include who was involved, and when, how often, and where events took place.

"Why" questions are usually best avoided. Young children are seldom able to formulate helpful answers, partly because their concepts of cause and effect are as yet poorly developed and partly because they sometimes tend to suggest blame or fault. Abused children should not be asked why they did not tell anyone; such questions tend to carry the implication that the child is at fault for not telling, and they seldom produce useful answers.

In middle childhood, the possibility of physical abuse can

usually be explored in the course of conversation. The topic is nevertheless a delicate one, and careful attention to the establishment of rapport is an important prerequisite. By this age children are usually acutely aware of the implications of disclosing abuse. They may know or at least suspect that the abuser may be charged, tried, and perhaps go to jail. If the abuser is a family member, especially if it is a parent, their statement may lead to the breakup of the family, perhaps the loss of their home and financial problems — for example, if the family's main wage earner goes to prison. They may fear further abuse as a result of their having "blown the whistle" on the abuser.

It is also difficult, and sometimes impossible, to reassure children when they entertain such fears and worries. All of the things above may indeed happen; in addition, the workings of the legal system are hard to predict. Abusing family members are not infrequently acquitted in court for a variety of technical legal reasons or because of conflicting evidence or questions about the credibility of evidence provided by children.

The situation is easier if the abuser is not a member of the family, especially if he or she is a stranger. Even so, conviction is not a certainty and the child may face long delays, interviews by a series of people, and then, perhaps, a harrowing experience of cross-examination in court. Interviews should be kept to a minimum as children often "close down" after they have been interviewed repeatedly.

It may be appropriate to discuss all these issues with older children and especially with adolescents. A straightforward, open and honest approach pays dividends. We cannot tell young people, with any degree of certainty, what will result from their disclosure of abuse. We can, however, tell them of the possibilities, assure them of our support in coping with the results of disclosure (if we are in a position to provide that support and are willing to do so), and even discuss with them the pros and cons of their revealing what has happened.

In dealing with adolescents, it is often best to get more

quickly to the point, especially if you have reason to believe they know why you are seeing them. It is particularly important that you explain to them what you will do with the information they give you. The confidentiality of these interviews is usually much less than that which applies in other situations and it is the duty of the interviewer to make this clear.

SEXUAL ABUSE

Much of what appears in the previous section applies also to cases of suspected sexual abuse. Yet there are differences. To many, the sexual exploitation of children is emotionally repulsive and arouses strong feelings. These feelings may be shared by sexually abused children. Many feel bad about themselves. They may feel that they are soiled, imperfect beings. They may believe that they are in important ways different from normal children or young people. They may feel that the abuse was in some way their fault (feelings which are also encountered in physically abused children, though seemingly with less intensity and frequency).

The sense of shame and unworthiness which some of these children have may make it hard for them to talk about what has occurred. The situation is especially difficult when the abusing person is a family member, for example the child's father or stepfather. The child's negative feelings may be mixed with feelings of love or affection for the father. The abuse may have started in the context of what appeared to be, and may have been, a loving, caring relationship. For a long time the daughter may have felt that she was someone chosen to have a special kind of relationship with her father. Indeed she may have been told this by the father. At times, moreover, the abusive behavior may have felt pleasant and may even have been enjoyed by the child. Revealing what happened may seem to the child like an act of betrayal. She may also feel powerless to do anything about the situation.

For all these reasons, interviews with sexually abused children, and those in whom abuse is suspected, require great clinical skill and sensitivity. The presence of well-developed rapport is essential and several interviews may be necessary before it is appropriate to start exploring issues of sexual abuse.

When you consider the time ripe for addressing the question of sexual abuse, you should do this gently, using open-ended questions and the child's own vocabulary. An excellent account of how to proceed is that of Jones and McQuiston (1988).

As with other clinical interviews, communication with younger subjects is mainly through play and other nonverbal channels. The use of dolls, whether anatomically correct or not, can greatly assist children, especially young ones, in explaining what they want to say. So can drawing. The examiner may draw a figure on a piece of paper or blackboard and invite the child to add to it. Some will proceed to indicate the parts where they have been touched or give other evidence of what has happened. Leading questions should be avoided as far as possible, though they may be permissible when they are designed to fill in details after abuse has been disclosed. Sometimes when open-ended questioning has revealed nothing and yet one still suspects that important information is being withheld, it may be better simply to wait and take the matter up at a later interview.

It is important that the interviewer respond appropriately to revelations of sexual (and other) abuse. It is sometimes difficult to avoid experiencing feelings of shock, disgust, or outrage at some of the acts of abuse perpetrated on children. Yet open expression of such feelings may cause the child to clam up or modify what he or she has to say. Statements made may even be retracted completely. A calm, matter-of-fact, and yet supportive attitude is usually best.

The use of "anatomically correct" dolls has come much into vogue in recent years. These are usually rag dolls with the genitalia, body orifices and hair all present. They are available in a wide variety of racial types and colors. While there are few study findings to indicate the extent to which the use of such dolls assists clinicians in investigating cases of possible sexual abuse, many interviewers find them useful. The child may be given the dolls to play with and talk about. White, Strom, Santilli, & Halpin, (1986) described a procedure for their use:

Identification of the dolls by sex and name.

Assessment of the child's knowledge of the body parts, sexual and nonsexual, by name and function.

"Private part knowledge."

"Abuse evaluation," consisting of asking the child about being touched, hurt, having secrets, receiving threats and other items which might indicate sexual abuse.

"Abuse elaboration," in which any "positive answers" to the previous questions are followed up.

There is a need for more standardization of the use of anatomically correct dolls and for more data on the responses of children who have not been abused. Jones and McQuiston (1988) are cautious in recommending the use of these dolls. They consider them "useful in certain circumstances, but [they] should not be the mainstay of all evaluative assessments of all young, potentially abused children." It seems, however, that the use of these dolls does not cause spurious reports of sexual abuse, and that they may be of particular value for use with "pre- and barely-verbal children when asking them to demonstrate abuse, and to provide a further medium through which a child of any age can describe abuse if she has already done so by words or using a drawing" (Jones & McQuiston, 1988, p. 34).

EMOTIONAL ABUSE

Emotional abuse often goes along with physical and/or sexual abuse, but it may occur without either. It is more difficult both to define and to identify. In essence, the emotionally abused child is one whose development has been adversely affected to a serious degree by the attitudes and handling of the parents. Although extreme cases of emotional abuse are obvious enough, drawing a clear line between emotional abuse and poor parenting is difficult, and exactly where we choose to draw it is arbitrary.

Garbarino et al. (1986), who use the term "emotionally battered child," describe five forms of "psychically destructive" behavior. These are:

> Rejecting: the child's worth and the legitimacy of his or her needs are not acknowledged by the adult.
>
> Isolating: the child is cut off by the adult from normal social experiences, prevented from forming frienships and made to believe that he or she is alone in the world.
>
> Terrorizing: the child is verbally assaulted by the adult who creates a climate of fear, bullies and frightens the child, and leads the child to believe the world is capricious and hostile.
>
> Ignoring: the child is deprived of needed stimulation and the adult fails to respond in suitable ways, stifling emotional growth and intellectual development.
>
> Corrupting: the child is "mis-socialized," being stimulated to engage in destructive antisocial behavior and reinforced in such deviant behavior.

While emotional abuse affects some children more than others, its principal effect is to diminish children's feelings of self-worth, while at the same time delaying social, intellectual and academic development.

When emotionally abused children are encountered in the course of clinical practice – and they are, alas, common – their poor views of themselves often become quickly evident. Sometimes the child's poor self-image is hidden behind a screen of bravado and it may be acted out in antisocial behavior of various kinds. We should always be on the lookout for these children. A child's self-esteem is of great importance. Many "negative" qualities can be reframed as desirable and our interviews with emotionally abused children provide opportunities for us to do so. For example, lying is generally thought of as an undesirable trait, but in a sense all the world's great storytellers, novelists and playwrights have been liars. The child who tells convincing lies may have a valuable talent which just needs to be applied in different contexts.

While undesirable traits and behavior may be reframed in ways such as the above, you should also be on the alert for indications of the child's talents and resources. Emotionally abused children are often unaware of these. Their abusing parents, or others, may have been so busy emphasizing the negative aspects of their personalities and behavior that the positive ones have been totally ignored.

Emotional abuse is frequently found in dysfunctional families. As we have seen, the borderline between "emotional abuse" and the kind of dysfunctional parenting commonly seen by child psychiatrists and other professionals working with disturbed children is hard to define. We must also remember that emotional abuse is not confined to families. It may occur in schools and in institutions of various sorts. The main issue is whether each child is regarded as a worthwhile person with his or her own unique talents, and whether the further development of those talents is fostered by all those concerned with the child's well-being.

SUMMARY

Child abuse – whether physical, sexual or emotional – is common and is increasingly being recognized. All who interview children in the course of their clinical work are liable to come across evidence of it. The conduct of interviews with children who may have been abused requires special skills. The usual rules of confidentiality may not apply and various legal issues may arise, including the necessity for the interviewer to report suspected abuse and the possibility that he or she may have to give evidence in court.

You should make sure that you have consent of the appropriate people to carry out the interview, and that all concerned are aware of the limits to confidentiality that apply.

It is essential to keep careful records. You should also be careful in framing questions, and avoid leading questions as far as possible.

The interaction between child and parents may suggest the existence of an abusive relationship. Younger children's play may also provide valuable revealing evidence. Children with adequate verbal skills may reveal the abuse through conversation. In cases of sexual abuse, the use of anatomically correct dolls may be of help.

Emotional abuse covers a wide range of damaging behaviors and attitudes which may be displayed by parents or guardians of children. Evidence of it may emerge in children's low self esteem and in retardation of their development in the social, emotional, or cognitive areas.

10

THE SUICIDAL CHILD

Suicide and suicidal behavior are unfortunately common, and seem to be getting more common in the adolescent populations of many countries. Recent years have also seen an increase in reports of suicidal behavior in younger children. While completed suicide is rare in middle childhood, suicidal ideation is not, and its presence is a frequent cause of referral of children for assessment. In adolescence, suicide is a leading cause of death, and suicidal behavior, which may or may not be accompanied by a real desire to die, frequently leads to requests that professionals in the mental health field interview young people.

Interviews with children and adolescents who may be suicidal should be based on the same principles as, and use techniques similar to, those described in earlier chapters. In addition there are some special considerations to be borne in mind when the assessment of suicidal risk is a particular aim of the interview. These will be the focus of this chapter.

THE CONTEXT OF THE INTERVIEW

A sense of urgency or fear is often present when possibly suicidal young people are referred. They require immediate attention and cannot be placed on a waiting list, such as exists in many mental health facilities, and left for weeks or months until their names come to the top of the list. They may present at hospital emergency departments, physicians' offices, or crisis centers of various sorts. If they have already made a suicide attempt, they may be seen in a hospital ward, perhaps after they have been resuscitated.

The urgency of these cases, and the short time line that must be adhered to in dealing with them, may make it difficult or impossible to follow the procedures set out earlier in this book to prepare the young person and the family for the interview. It may not be possible to contact and obtain information from relatives. Little or no past history, apart from what the person being interviewed is able to provide, may be available. These interviews are seldom carefully planned and may not take place in the interviewer's usual office or clinic setting. The facilities available in hospital emergency departments and wards for mental health interviews vary and are by no means uniformly satisfactory.

Thus, not only is the issue to be addressed a particularly serious one – perhaps even one of life and death – but the conditions for the interview may be less than optimal. Furthermore, the motivation of the young person who is to be interviewed may be suspect. The interview may have been requested by a third person, be it relative, other professional, or friend, the subject having little or no desire to have his or her state of mind assessed.

The time factor also imposes some constraints. Suicidal clients appear at unpredictable and often inconvenient times (late on a Friday afternoon seems to be a favorite one!). Working under pressure, as is often the case, the clinician may be be hard pressed to give the suicidal young person the careful, measured consideration required.

Since these are important cases, rather than rushing into seeing these patients in time "borrowed" from others or between appointments, I prefer to wait until I have adequate time available and can give my unhurried and undivided attention to the young person concerned. This may mean waiting until the end of the working day; it may not be to the liking of emergency room staff, but carrying out a proper assessment must be given a high priority.

GATHERING BACKGROUND INFORMATION

When a child is referred for assessment of suicidal risk, it is important to discover the reasons why this issue has been raised. Has there been a previous or recent attempt at suicide? Has the young person been threatening suicide? Has a suicide note been found? Has there been a recent suicide in the child's family or social circle? Has the child appeared depressed? If there have been previous attempts, how serious have they been? Is there any history of alcohol or drug use or abuse?

Any available family or social history should also be obtained. Is there any reason to believe that the young person has been faced with stressful situations at home, in school or elsewhere? How did the young person's case come to the attention of whoever is seeking the assessment? In summary, the more the interviewer knows about the subject's background, the better the assessment of the case is likely to be.

It may not be possible to get this information from the patient. Sometimes depressed individuals, especially those who entertain a strong wish to die, falsify their accounts of events or of their current state of mind.

THE INTERVIEW

Preparations for the interview should follow the usual lines; the establishment of rapport is at least as important in interviewing suicidal children as it is in other clinical situations. It is usually advisable to explore other areas before getting round to the key areas of depression and suicidal ideation and intent. However, a brief initial discussion of the reasons for the interview and its possible objectives is usually in order.

It helps to obtain first a general history, which includes the young person's age, school grade or work status, family background, past medical and psychiatric history, and current and recent life situation – for example, place of abode, with whom the young person is living, and the stability of the social context.

If there have been no previous attempts at suicide, the young person's mental state should be explored with particular reference to whether there is evidence of current depression. Careful inquiry should also be made for any past history of depression.

Many young people do not have a clear understanding of what we mean by depression. This should be explained in terms of feeling low, sad, like crying, and perhaps not wanting to live. If the young person ackowledges having, or having had, such feelings, it is then necessary to inquire about duration and intensity. We have all of us experienced feelings of depression from time to time. If these feelings have been brief, lasting perhaps a few hours with longer periods of normal mood in between, they may be normal reactions to stressful events. This is especially so if they have occurred in association with stress, rejection, or failure in some endeavor. Clinical depression persists even though those unhappy events are long past. Nevertheless, environmental stress is often present and may be an important contributory factor in the genesis of the depressive state.

Various other symptoms often accompany depression. Since sleep disturbance is a common one, it is important to inquire about changes in sleep patterns. Sleep may be disrupted by early morning waking, by repeated waking during the night, or by difficulty in getting to sleep. Meanwhile the subject may feel sleepy and lacking in energy during the day; yet when bedtime comes restful sleep eludes the person. There may also be appetite changes; these may take the form of either decreased or increased appetite, accompanied also by weight changes. Concentration may be poor; in fact, an early sign of depression is often a sudden drop in the level of the young person's school or work performance. Psychomotor retardation – the slowing down of thought processes and motor activity – may accompany the more severe forms of depression.

The severity of depression may be investigated in various

ways. You may ask the patient to rate it on a scale of one to ten, ten being very severe, with no desire to continue living, while one is a slight deviation from the subject's normal mood. I do not find this approach particularly helpful. If a semi-objective measure is desired, it is probably better to use some device such as the Beck Depression Inventory or other self-report instrument.

It is usually more helpful to explore questions such as, "Have you ever felt so low that you thought life was not worth living?" or, "Have you actually wished you were dead?" If such questions are answered in the affirmative, the next question might be, "Have you actually thought of harming or killing yourself?" If the answer is again yes, one should then ask more specific questions, such as, "What did you consider doing?" If the subject has reached the stage of forming specific suicide plans, it is important to ascertain what these have been. This enables the clinician to assess how likely it is that the implementation of the plans would lead to the person's death. It is also helpful to ask what has stopped the young person from carrying out the plans. The reasons given may vary from religious ones to the distress the subject would cause to others. They may also reveal elements of hope and ambivalent feelings about death.

When a history of suicidal ideation is established, you should also inquire as to how recently these thoughts were entertained, under what circumstances they appeared and were most prominent, and how severe and persistent they have been. Do they occur only when the subject is facing a lot of stress or are they experienced at other times? Whether or not the young person has future plans may also give an indication of how serious the risk of suicide is. The subject who expresses a wish to be dead, yet is looking forward to participating in a successful season as a member of a sports team, or talks enthusiastically of the family's forthcoming vacation, may be at less risk than one who has no such plans or hopes.

If the young person has actually attempted suicide or has displayed behavior which might be construed as suicidal, it is necessary to go into this in detail. I try to get as full an account as possible of the events leading up to the attempt. Was the event planned or was it impulsive? Was the use of alcohol or other drugs involved? What did the young person think would happen as a result of the suicidal act? Was there a strong desire to die? If not, what was the motive? In many cases suicidal behavior is a cry for help, intended to draw attention to the subject's distress or plight rather than to end one's life.

It is also helpful to consider why the attempt was unsuccessful. Did the subject inform someone of the act (for example by telling a friend or family member that he or she had taken an overdose of sleeping tablets) in time for resuscitation to be carried out?

As a general rule, the risk of suicide is greater when the subject has been getting steadily more depressed over a period of time. It also becomes greater as the subject has less communication with others. The isolated depressed person is especially at risk, particularly when communication with others has recently broken down. A long history of self-injurious behavior indicates a poorer prognosis. The extent to which suicidal behavior has been intended as a means of communication, and whether the communication has been heeded by those to whom it was directed, should also be explored. Most serious of all are suicidal acts performed in isolation, especially when accompanied by a strong desire to die.

PARASUICIDE

"Parasuicide" is a term sometimes applied to minor and relatively nonlethal self-injurious acts which do not appear to be intended to cause the death of the subject. These include such acts as wrist-slashing, other forms of self-mutilation, and the taking of small quantities of painkillers or other drugs. Parasuicidal acts are often carried out in the presence of others or in situations where detection is likely to follow quickly. Indeed, they are frequently intended to draw attention to the subject.

Parasuicide is much commoner than completed suicide in teenage girls whereas the reverse holds true for teenage boys. The latter are more prone to major, and successful, suicidal acts (Hawton, O'Grady, Osborn, & Cole, 1982).

Although parasuicide seldom leads to death (though this occasionally happens as a result of a miscalculation), it should nevertheless be taken seriously. We should conduct an interview along the same lines as recommended for suicidal subjects generally. Parasuicidal behavior usually results from serious emotional or personality problems and can be understood as a cry for some form of help. In many such cases, a full psychiatric assessment may be advisable once the immediate crisis has been dealt with. While in many cases parasuicide does not lead to actual suicide, it may do so if the message the young person is trying to convey is not heeded.

A full, in-depth discussion of the subject's situation is necessary in all cases, whether of serious suicide attempt, parasuicide, or suicidal ideation. It is important to explore the issues in the young person's life behind the wish to die or the self-injurious behavior that has occurred. Such a discussion usually leads to the recommendation of an appropriate treatment plan.

THE YOUNGER SUICIDAL CHILD

In the past it has been said that suicide is rare before puberty. Shaffer (1974), obtained information about all the recorded suicides in children aged 10 to 14 in England and Wales over a seven-year period, and found none below the age of 12. While completed suicide is certainly rare before puberty, it is not unknown, and suicidal behavior—threats of suicide or self-destructive talk or behavior—is by no means uncommon. Pfeffer, Zuckerman, Plutchkin, and Mizruchi (1984) found that of 101 children aged 6 to 12 (mean age 9.7), randomly selected from a school (though one serving children of poor socioeconomic status), 11.9 percent reported suicidal ideas, threats or attempts. Three had made attempts at suicide.

Myers, Burke, and McCauley (1985) report that 61 (17.5 percent—40 boys and 21 girls) of 348 children aged 5–13 admitted to a psychiatric unit had engaged in suicidal behavior; this was defined as "any self-destructive statement or action expressed with explicit desire to kill oneself, and offered either spontaneously or upon interview." A wish to be dead did not qualify. Seven of these children were aged 5 to 7, and 25 were in the age range 8 to 10. Some other studies of child psychiatric populations have shown higher rates of suicidal behavior.

Clearly we cannot ignore the possibility of suicidal ideation, even in children as young as five, and we should inquire further into such ideas. One thing we should attempt to discover is what the child understands death to be. Many younger children do not understand the finality of death, and their concept of what it means to die may differ markedly from that of older children and adolescents. In fairy tales, in television cartoons, and in other forms of fiction people may appear to die and then come back to life.

Another point to investigate is how the child became acquainted with the idea of suicide. In my own clinical practice I have found that in such cases there has often been talk of suicide, or there have actually been one or more suicides, in the child's family or social circle. There may be a parent or an older sibling who is in the habit of threatening or even attempting suicide, and the young child may have learned this behavior by imitation. This is especially likely if the other person's suicidal behavior is perceived as having some value or leading to some advantage, such as getting others to give in to the person's demands or wishes. It is therefore usually worthwhile to ask the child if anyone else in the family has threatened suicide or has talked of wanting to die. If they have, one can ask what happened as a result.

Investigating these points, both in conversation and in play, can assist the interviewer in understanding the family dynamics as well as in discovering how serious the risk of suicide is.

SUMMARY

Suicide and suicidal behavior are common in adolescents. In younger children suicidal behavior is frequently encountered, though completed suicide is quite rare.

As much background information as possible should be obtained before interviewing suicidal subjects, but in many cases only limited information is available. These interviews are often requested by those who urgently need help, and may take place in hospital emergency departments or wards or other institutional settings, rather than the interviewer's usual place of work. A careful, unhurried exploration of the young person's situation is necessary. So also is asessment of whether there has been or remains a clear wish to die. The severity of any associated depression must be evaluated.

Parasuicide, the performance of minor and relatively non-lethal self-injurious acts, also merits careful inquiry along similar lines. Although the risk of death may be low, there are often serious emotional or personality problems behind the behavior. Younger children with suicidal ideation often come from families with serious problems in the family dynamics.

11

SPECIAL CLINICAL SITUATIONS

THE NONSPEAKING CHILD

For a variety of reasons children may not talk when interviewed. It may be that they have not yet acquired verbal language skills. It may be due to their age or generally delayed cognitive development, as in mentally retarded children. It may also be a feature of certain specific handicaps such as deafness, developmental language disorders, or pervasive developmental disorders.

Children who cannot speak must be distinguished from those who refuse to do so even though they have the ability to talk. The latter group include some psychotic and otherwise severely disturbed children and those with the condition known as "elective mutism."

CHILDREN WHO HAVE NOT YET ACQUIRED SPEECH

Some approaches to children who have not acquired speech, either because of their young age or because of mental retardation, have been discussed in Chapters 7 and 8. Similar considerations apply to those who have not acquired speech because of deafness or developmental language disorders, though there are some important differences we should bear in mind when dealing with each of these groups.

Deaf children are usually of normal intelligence and their nonverbal communication skills may be excellent; in this respect they differ from mentally retarded children whose nonverbal abilities are usually affected to much the same degree as their verbal ones. Some deaf subjects are expert lip-readers and others have learned to communicate in sign language. The professional who works regularly with deaf children might do well to learn sign language. Quite sophisticated communication with older and cognitively more able deaf children may be possible through writing. Such children are often particularly skilled in using other sensory channels, especially sight and touch. Play, drawing, painting and modeling therefore assume even greater importance when one is interviewing a deaf child than in work with children with normal hearing.

Developmental language disorders are conditions in which the acquisition of verbal language skills is delayed, despite normal or relatively normal development of other psychological functions. As with deafness and mental retardation, the delay may only be one of degree and the child may have some speech.

Language has both receptive and expressive functions. Some children's receptive language skills are relatively good, while their expressive skills are less well developed. Some children may even be able to understand what others say normally for their age, their handicap being confined to expressing themselves verbally. Nonverbal communication may be normal or it may be disproportionately well developed in children with developmental language disorders, as is also often the case with deaf children. Being forced to rely on nonverbal means of expressing themselves, many of these children acquire greater facility in using those channels of communication that are open to them.

Whether or not assessment of the child's communication skills is one of the primary objectives of your interview, it is important always to consider them. This will guide you as you proceed; in particular, it will tell you how much you must rely on nonverbal communication.

Many of the points made in Chapter 8 are relevant in dealing with the severely language-delayed child. Thus neutral questions are in order until the interviewer is able to form an assessemnt of the level of the child's verbal skills. As with mentally retarded children, the use of body language, including gestures and facial expressions, should be emphasized, as should nonverbal activities such as play, painting, drawing, and modeling. The main difference between mentally retarded and language-delayed children is that, in the latter group, other aspects of cognitive development, as well as emotional and social development, may be proceeding normally. We should keep this important point in mind. With these children, as with others who suffer from handicaps, especially those that involve communication, one must guard against the danger of "talking down" to them. This very real danger is best avoided by a careful consideration of the ability level of the child disregarding the communication handicap.

Pervasive developmental disorders include autistic disorders and some other severe abnormalities of the development of a wide range of psychological functions. These conditions are discussed more fully in *Basic Child Psychiatry* (Barker, 1988, Chapter 7). Their main features, as set out in the revised version of the third edition of the American Psychiatric Association's *Diagnostic and Statistical Manual (DSM-III-R)* (American Psychiatric Association, 1987), are:

Qualitative impairment of reciprocal social interaction.
Impairment of communication and imaginative activity.
A markedly restricted repertoire of activities and interests.

These are socially withdrawn children who seem to lack empathy for others and are content to engage for long periods in repetitive, stereotyped activities of a mechanical nature. Their speech development is delayed and abnormal and some never develop any meaningful speech. Echolalia, the repetition of words or phrases spoken by others rather than giving a meaningful reply, is common.

These children tend to resist change in their environment.

Their capacity for abstract thought is severely limited and they usually fail to engage in symbolic play. When they do play with toys they seldom use them for their symbolic function. For instance, an autistic child may not use a toy telephone to speak into or for a "pretend" conversation, but is more likely to use it as a rattle or to bang it on the floor.

The onset of autistic disorders is usually during the first two or three years of life, but many of these children have displayed abnormal development from birth. More than half suffer from a moderate or severe degree of mental retardation in addition to autism. The causes of autistic disorders are not fully understood, though biological factors appear to be important in the genesis of the profound abnormalities of function that these children display. Genetic factors are certainly involved, at least in some cases. Chromosome abnormalities, notably the "fragile X" syndrome, are present more often in autistic children than in the general population (Gillberg & Wahlstrom, 1985; Fisch, Cohen, Wolf, Brown, Jenkins, & Gross, 1986). Autistic disorders are three times commoner in boys than in girls.

Communicating with an autistic child presents the interviewer with a challenge. Being aware of the condition and recognizing it when it is encountered is a good first step. It is then necessary to devise some way of entering the child's world. Nonverbal means are the best way to achieve this. In every case the approach must be developed according to the particular child's characteristics. Many autistic children engage in repetitive motor activities such as rocking to and fro, or from side to side, on their feet. With a boy who is doing this you might take hold of his hands and initially rock to and fro in rhythm with his movements. This is but an example of the "pacing" we discussed in Chapter 3. The next step might be to modify the rate or rhythm of the movements, so that you begin to take control. Following that you might try initiating different movements – perhaps side-to-side movements if the boy normally engages in to-and-fro rocking.

By means such as the above, it becomes possible to gain an idea of the child's relationship capacity. Such activities may lead to other forms of reciprocal play, for example, simple games like "pat-a-cake." How much can be achieved is an important diagnostic point, since impairment of reciprocal social interaction is, as we have seen, a major feature of these disorders.

Many autistic children have particular areas of relative, sometimes remarkable, strength. For example, they may have great musical talents, an exceptional memory, or great facility at mathematics. Such talents can often be used in establishing communication. If the child appears to have a good musical ear and enjoys listening to music, dancing or rocking to it may be ways into the child's world. Developing musical games or dances may then be ways of making further contact with the child.

As they get older many autistic children develop preoccupations with particular activities or subjects. They may pore over maps or bus or train timetables and become familiar with these to an extraordinary degree. One autistic boy knew the numbers of all the major, and most of the minor, highways in Britain. You had only to ask him how to get from one town or city to another and he would correctly reel off the numbers of the highways you would have to take. I found that a good way of establishing initial contact with this boy was to discuss highway routes and the travels I had undertaken on Britain's roads.

Finally, it is important to be persistent in dealing clinically with autistic children. Initially, and perhaps for a long while afterwards, they will resist your attempts to communicate with them. You should not be put off by such responses. Persistence, combined with a flexible approach that explores the best way of establishing communication, usually pays off eventually. The process is very much one of trial and error. Since there is no one formula to use with these children, it is necessary to establish a specific strategy for each child. Even tiny gains can be the start of meaningful communication. Until a variety of strategies has each been given a good trial, we should not "write off" any of these children as unable to enter into meaningful communication with us.

THE CHILD WHO REFUSES TO SPEAK

Refusal to speak is seen in its most striking form in "elective mutism." It may also be encountered in some psychotic children and adolescents, in some children with severe conduct disorders, and occasionally in severely depressed subjects. Psychotic disorders are discussed in the following section.

Elective mutism is a puzzling but well recognized condition. The child declines to speak in certain situations while speaking in others. The refusal to speak is often determined and persistent. Most frequently these children speak at home but not at school or in other situations away from home – for example, in the clinics and offices of mental health professionals. Nevertheless it is known that they are able to speak. Indeed, they may, even in a clinical setting, talk freely with family members until an outsider, such as a member of the clinic staff, enters the room. Then they clam up.

Elective mutism, at least in its more severe forms, is quite rare. Brown and Lloyd (1975), in a survey of 6,072 children starting elementary school in Birmingham, England, found that 42 were still not speaking in class after eight weeks in school, a prevalence rate of 7.2 per thousand. But the rate fell steadily during subsequent months so that after 64 weeks only one child remained silent in school. Thus, while mutism is fairly common as an initial reaction to starting school, it is much rarer as a persisting phenomenon. According to Kolvin and Fundudis (1981), the prevalence in eight-year-olds is probably about 0.8 per thousand.

There is no easy prescription for getting electively mute children to speak in those situations in which they elect not to do so. Many strategies have been suggested but none is universally successful and most of these children stubbornly resist attempts to get them to speak, often over many months or even several years.

Not only is verbal communication with these children difficult, but many of them also resist communicating by nonverbal means such as play. Some will come passively into the interview room, even declining the invitation to sit down. They similarly may decline to play, draw or paint, as well as failing to respond to questions.

For our purposes, the important thing is to be aware of this condition and recognize it when it is encountered. The interviewer usually has to be content with observing the reactions of the child to the various phases of the interview process. These may amount to a series of passive responses. In such cases, obtaining a good history from parents, teachers and others who know the child in different situations is imperative. The responses the child gives when interviewed, passive as they are, then confirm the diagnosis. Further information on elective mutism is to be found in *Basic Child Psychiatry* (Barker, 1988, Chapter 11).

Some *severely behaviorally disturbed children* decline to speak when interviewed. Most suffer from conditions falling into the categories of "conduct disorder" and "oppositional defiant disorder", as defined in DSM-III-R (American Psychiatric Association, 1987). In my experience it is more common for parents or other involved adults to report that the young person (it is more often an adolescent than a child) has stated his or her intention not to talk in the interview than it is for this behavior actually to be displayed when the young person is being interviewed. Some young people decline to talk during family interviews but open up and speak freely when seen on their own.

When conduct disordered or delinquent children refuse to speak, this is usually a manifestation of angry feelings either toward the adult world generally or toward the parents and those seen as allied to the parents (as helping professionals are often seen). The anger can usually be understood in the light of the child's history and the past and current family dynamics. The hostility the child displays towards the interviewer is often displaced anger originating in the relationship the child has with the parents or a stepparent or other adult.

Careful, persistent and patient use of the various rapport-building techniques discussed in Chapter 3 will usually help overcome these young people's reluctance to talk. It is important also to explain carefully your role, the confidentiality of the interview, and, perhaps, your understanding of the young person's anger as being the result of years of frustration (if this appears to be the case). Once young people begin to feel that you are on their side, rather than being agents of their parents or other authority figures, they usually begin to talk.

In many of these clinical situations it is helpful to point out to these children that they do not have to tell you anything they don't want to, and that if there are topics they want to rule out of order altogether you will respect this. These statements are, as we saw earlier, truisms, since we cannot force children to reveal information they do not want to give us. But the reassurance that we will not try and the statement that we wish to respect their wishes and their right to keep information to themselves often result in their becoming willing to talk. As the interviewer comes to be seen as nonthreatening, empathic, and concerned with the young person's welfare, as well as with his or her opinions, the reluctance to talk often melts away.

Severe degrees of depression may be associated with psychomotor retardation – the slowing of thought processes and motor activities – which, in its extreme form, may amount to a total failure to speak. "Depressive stupor" is an even more extreme state in which the patient fails to respond at all. When failure to speak is a manifestation of a severe depressive disorder, the latter is usually clearly apparent once a history has been taken from the relatives and the clinical state of the patient has been observed. Following effective treatment of the depression, communication may be expected to return to normal. The important thing in these cases is to ensure prompt treatment for the depression, rather than persistently trying to get the person to talk. The diagnosis and treatment of depressive disorders are discussed in *Basic Child Psychiatry* (Barker, 1988, Chapter 6).

Finally, it is worth mentioning that a person's refusal or

reluctance to talk during an interview is itself a valuable piece of clinical information. It is usually a manifestation of a serious problem which requires some form of skilled intervention.

THE PSYCHOTIC CHILD

Until quite recently infantile autism and related conditions were classified as psychotic conditions. This is misleading, since they are primarily severe disorders of the development of various cognitive, social, and emotional skills. Psychoses, on the other hand, are defined as disorders in which there is a loss of contact with the real world where the subject is living. The psychotic person is attempting to adjust to a subjectively distorted concept of reality. Psychotic disorders of childhood and adolescence fall into four groups:

Schizophrenia.
Disintegrative psychoses, in many of which there is organic disease of the brain; the organic process may be progressive or nonprogressive.
Reactive psychoses.
Toxic confusional and delirious states, which are associated with acute infections, metabolic disorders and other general disorders, or with intoxication by drugs.

It is not possible here to go fully into the diagnosis of the above categories of psychosis. For this, textbooks of psychiatry should be consulted. The causes, presentation and treatment of these conditions are also discussed further in *Basic Child Psychiatry* (Barker, 1988, Chapter 8). Nevertheless anyone whose work involves interviewing young people may from time to time be faced with a child or adolescent who appears out of touch with reality or whose thinking processes seem seriously disordered – as is the case with many psychotic individuals. In such cases, it may be wise to seek confirmation of the suspected diagnosis through consultation with a psychiatrist or other specialist.

As an interview with a psychotic patient proceeds, the clinician is likely to become aware of the patient's distorted view of reality. Sometimes, however, it may not be easy to determine whether or not the subject's statements are based on delusional (that is objectively false) beliefs. Thus some patients' paranoid delusions that various people are persecuting them in a variety of ways and that there is a plot being hatched against them may sound quite convincing. Moreover, people are sometimes persecuted in real life. It may therefore be necessary to check with others and obtain a history from those who know the patient as part of the assessment of such patients.

Hallucinations (the subjective experience of sensory perceptions which do not arise from the external world) are present in many psychoses. Auditory hallucinations (hearing voices) are particularly characteristic of schizophrenia. Visual hallucinations are more characteristic of organic psychoses.

In interviewing children in whom a psychotic process is suspected, we must distinguish between delusions and fantasies. Delusions are beliefs that are firmly held regardless of the objective reality of the subject's situation. Fantasies are fanciful, imaginative ideas which the subject knows are not real. Many children have active fantasy lives in which they may get deeply involved. Yet they are aware that what they are into is "play" or "pretend" or "a game." They can distinguish the people, situations, and activities of their fantasy world from the real world around them. Careful questioning by the interviewer may be necessary to establish that this is the case. This is often a major issue in one's interviews with such children.

Sometimes it quickly becomes apparent that a child is psychotic. The child may be obviously out of touch with reality. This applies to many cases of organic psychoses (those due to diseases of the brain) and to those in which a generalized disorder (for example, a severe infection or a metabolic disorder such as diabetic ketoacidosis) causes a confusional state. In such cases, patients may be obviously disoriented for time, place, and person. They may not know who those around them are, even if these are familiar figures. Because of this, it may be impossible to establish any real contact with them. Extensive interviews with children with acute and severe organic psychoses are seldom necessary. The presence of an underlying causative condition is usually clear and the immediate need is for the diagnosis and treatment of the underlying physical disease. Recovery from this is usually accompanied by a return to normal of the patient's mental state.

Psychotic states can also be induced by the abuse of drugs, either "street" drugs such as marihuana, other cannabis products, lysergic acid diethyamide ("acid"), cocaine, or opiates; or pharmacological preparations taken in excessive doses. A fuller list of drugs commonly abused by young people appears in *Basic Child Psychiatry* (Barker, 1988, page 257), and drugs of abuse are discussed more fully by Blum (1984). Young people whose mental states are seriously disordered may be seen in hospital emergency departments and in other settings for young people in crisis. We must always keep in mind the possibility that their disturbed mental states may be due to the illicit use of drugs. Therefore, during clinical interviews with such individuals it is especially important to explore their use of any type of drug.

Psychotic states due to cerebral or other diseases or to drugs are typically accompanied by altered states of consciousness. The patient is disoriented as well as having delusional ideas, hallucinations, and other signs of a psychotic process. On the other hand, in the so-called "functional" psychoses such as schizophrenia, psychotic symptoms occur in a setting of clear consciousness. Understanding and correctly assessing such patients can be particularly challenging. In interviewing them some of the approaches recommended above for use with autistic children are often helpful.

Just as it is necessary to enter the fantasy lives of young children in order to understand them properly, so also do we need to enter the psychotic child's world. Techniques such as play, the use of puppets, drawing and painting, conversation, and telling stories, can all help us enter the world of the psychotic child. It is not usually helpful, at least not in interviews designed to establish a diagnosis and contribute to a general understanding of a case, to deny the young person his or her psychotic world or delusional beliefs. You may want to challenge such beliefs to discover how firmly they are held, and it can also be helpful to see what the patient's reaction is to a reasoned argument that questions the validity of the possibly delusional ideas. A careful balance must be kept between testing out how firmly the child holds the beliefs and is impervious to evidence that casts doubt on them, on the one hand, and accepting the child's beliefs and working, for the moment, on the basis that they are valid.

SUMMARY

Children who do not speak at interview include those who have not yet acquired verbal language skills and those who, though able to speak, choose not to do so. In interviewing the former, we rely on nonverbal methods of communication such as play, drawing, painting, and the use of puppets. When interviewing the latter group, careful attention to the establishment of rapport may overcome the young person's unwillingness to speak. In elective mutism, however, the refusal to speak may be prolonged and determined.

Communication with nonspeaking autistic children and those with other pervasive developmental disorders has to start with involvement in whatever activities the child displays. These may be primitive motor activities such as rocking. Communication can often be developed from this basis.

Severely depressed children may not speak in interviews, but effective treatment of the depression usually leads to a resumption of normal communication.

Establishing communication with psychotic children usually requires that the interviewer enter, at least in some measure, the world of the child. This process is similar to that of entering the world of the autistic child. Not until communication is well established should the psychotic child's delusional beliefs be directly challenged.

12

TERMINATION AND OTHER ISSUES

TERMINATION

We have discussed in Chapters 4 and 6 the termination of individual interviews, but we need also to consider how to end a series of interviews. Children who have been interviewed repeatedly, whatever the objectives of the interviews may have been, are liable to become emotionally attached to the interviewer. Most series of interviews have therapeutic or counseling aims, so that emotional issues have likely been highlighted.

Skillfully conducted interviews by empathic clinicians have the potential to be of real therapeutic value, even if they have not been labeled as psychotherapy. They may provide personal affirmation of the subject being interviewed. The experience of being accepted in an uncritical and non-judgmental way by a caring adult is new to some children. Such acceptance may be hard to give up when the interviews have to end. Another point is that interviews with children can be, and ideally should be, fun for all concerned. In my experience this is often the case — and few children want to give up doing something which is fun.

What I have written elsewhere (Barker, 1986, p. 248) about terminating therapy with families applies equally to individuals. Thus the ending of therapy may be a time of great emotional significance. It may, consciously or unconsciously, remind the person of previous separations or losses. Inexpertly managed, it can appear to clients as a rejection, but, just as the death of a loved one can be the occasion to celebrate that person's life and achievements, so can the ending of treatment be an occasion to celebrate what has been achieved. Nevertheless we must always be on the lookout for signs that termination is proving difficult for the children we see. As Lankton and Lankton (1983, p. 345) put it:

> The business of other "goodbyes" may be revived. These may have nothing to do with the expressed purpose of the therapy but nevertheless be stimulated by the parallel situation.

It is of course not true that all children enjoy being interviewed. Some sullen or angry young people – more often adolescents than younger children – are delighted when a series of interviews comes to an end. They may have been attending under some sort of duress, for example, a probation order requiring them to have therapy or counseling, and are glad when they are done with the requirement. In an ideal world, these clients would have been "seduced" into an active and constructive therapeutic relationship during the course of their interviews, but this outcome may not be achieved. If so, termination is a rather different experience.

How the termination process is planned and conducted will depend, among other things, on the nature of the relationship that has developed between interviewer and child, the period of time over which interviews have been occurring, the reasons for the termination, and whether there is the possibility of any further contact between interviewer and child. The child's observed reaction to the pending termination must also be taken into account. Nevertheless some general guidelines may be helpful:

Giving notice and *mentioning from time to time* the forthcoming ending of a series of interviews is always important. The importance grows in proportion to the length of the series and the intensity of the relationship that has developed between interviewer and young person. Mention of the forthcoming termination may provoke expressions of anxiety, sadness, feeling abandoned or anticipated loss. When this happens it is a sign that unresolved issues remain to be dealt with in therapy. When treatment is near to a successful conclusion, however, the response of the young person to the mention of termination is usually an expression of pleasure that the work that had to be done is nearing completion.

Sometimes the duration of the therapy or counseling, or the number of sessions that is planned, is known in advance. This makes the termination process a little simpler, though not necessarily any easier for the young person. As a general rule, I like to start foreshadowing the ending of the interviews about two-thirds of the way through the series. This can also have therapeutic advantages. For instance, it gives notice that there is a limited time during which the aims of the interview series must be achieved. When interviews have therapeutic objectives, as many do, this may help focus the therapy process on the relevant issues. This applies especially to older children and adolescents, as well as to adults.

Determining what is to happen when the interviews come to an end is a necessary prerequisite for termination. The interviewer should know, well in advance if possible, whether the ending of the interviews will also be the conclusion of the clinical services the child is to receive, or whether some other service, perhaps provided by another professional, will be offered. Does the ending of the interviews mark a move from a residential setting back home? Or is it part of a move of service from one agency to another? Is it occurring because you yourself are moving to another position, agency or city? In many cases the answers to such questions will have been negotiated ahead of time with parents or guardians, and ideally with involvement also of the child.

Whatever the answers to these and other relevant questions, the child should know who there will be in his or her life who can play, at least in some measure, a role similar to that the interviewer has played. This usually needs to be done in conjunction with the child's family and whoever referred the child in the first place. In many cases, the child's care will be returned to the referrer. It may be that no further treatment is likely to be needed and the child will simply remain in the parents' care.

The final interview should deal primarily or entirely with termination issues. I like to review the whole series of interviews, starting with the circumstances under which the child was referred, surveying the course of the interviews and reviewing the progress that has been made. If the series has been a long one, I will have previously reviewed progress in similar ways from time to time and the process can be similar. I encourage the child's feedback on what has occurred and make it clear that I want to learn as much as I can from the review. When seeing older children and adolescents, I tell them that I am still learning and that what they tell me may enable me to help others more effectively in the future.

I believe that the final interview should be a sharing of the experiences child and interviewer have had together. It may be a time to focus both on the high spots and on the low ones, and then to look forward to a brighter future.

I prefer to be optimistic about the future prospect. The question of how far one should discuss possible future problems, or the recurrence of previous ones, is difficult. One should, of course, be prepared for these and know how to handle them. But dwelling too much on what may go wrong in the future can leave the child with the feeling that you are expecting this to happen; it could even turn out to be a self-fulfilling prophesy. One way to deal with this dilemma is to emphasize the strengths the child has acquired during the course of the interviews, and how these will be safeguards against the recurrence of problems.

Another difficult question is whether one should say that one is available to provide further help if it is needed—if, of course, you would be a position to do so. This may be reassuring but it may also imply that you expect that there will or may be further problems. There are ways in which the possibility of offering further help can be mentioned, while implying that you do not think it will be needed. For example one might say, "I don't expect I'll need to see you again, but you know where I am if you ever want a chat," or something along those lines.

On the whole I prefer to avoid statements such as the above, unless the young person asks whether it will be possible to come back if he or she wants. In the latter case we should explore what it is that the young person feels might lead to a need to return.

A possible way of dealing with the question of further contacts is to propose a "follow-up" contact or contacts — something I often do. This consists of getting in touch with child and/or family, usually by telephone, perhaps three months or at some other interval(s) of time, after the interview series ends. The options are to ask the child or family to call you or to make a note to call them. You can prepare the child or family by saying, "I always like to know how the people I have been seeing are doing after they stop seeing me, so I'll give you a call in three months or so." It is important to make it clear that this is a routine procedure, not one proposed for this particular child or family.

Finally, I believe it is important to thank the child for the opportunity I have had to share in his or her life. Clinical work is not a one-way process. We learn much from those we interview. Indeed most of what we know and use in our clinical work has probably been learned from those we have worked with in the past. It is quite appropriate to point this out in the final session — and perhaps also at other times during the course of therapy.

INTERRUPTIONS

Much of what applies to the termination of a series of interviews, especially those of a therapeutic nature, applies also to interruptions to the series. Interruptions may result from illness in child or family, illness affecting the interviewer, vacations, family crises such as serious illnesses or death of a family member, the incarceration of the young person in an institution, or a move to a different area by child or interviewer. Some of these circumstances may perforce lead to termination but many need not.

If it is known in advance that a planned series of interviews will have to be interrupted for any reason, it is advisable to inform all concerned and discuss this with them. This may help lessen or avoid feelings of rejection or loss the child might otherwise feel. If the interruption is one that could not have been predicted, as when it is due to illness, we should take the earliest opportunity to discuss and explain the reasons to the young person. This may be done by telephone or by a third person, such as a professional colleague or parent, if the interviewer is unable to do it. When the interviews are resumed the interruption and the child's feelings about it should be explored and dealt with.

If the interruption occurs because the family is moving to another city, every effort should be made to find the child a similar service in the new location, if that is what the family wishes. If it is the interviewer who is moving or is unable to continue the interviews for any other reason, he or she has the responsibility of finding an appropriate professional to take over the work. The process to be gone through with the child is similar to that of termination.

KEEPING RECORDS OF INTERVIEWS

Keeping accurate and up-to-date records of what we do is important in all clinical work. Many clinics, institutions and agencies have policies regarding the recording of clinical work but even if we are working on our own in private practice it is an ethical imperative that we keep good records.

There are many reasons why we should keep scrupulously accurate and current records. We must be able to refer back to the work we have done previously without having to rely upon memory. Unless one has a photographic memory, which few do, it is impossible to remember everything that has happened in each interview. The larger one's practice the more this applies. Reviewing one's notes of previous sessions is always helpful, especially when the progress of therapy seems to have come to a stop. Good records are also invaluable when the time comes for the termination of a series of interviews.

A good record of your interviews may be needed for use by colleagues, for example when you are absent on vacation or for any other reason. In much clinical work it is important that whoever is standing in for you when you are away has access to information about the work you are doing. We may also be asked, perhaps years later, to provide reports on interviews we have conducted, at the request of former clients who may now be seeking help from another professional or agency.

There are also legal reasons for keeping good clinical records. Malpractice actions are increasingly being launched against professionals of all sorts, and we may also be called to account by the licensing authorities governing our practice. Good clinical records are among our best defenses against adverse allegations concerning our practice. (They are of course no substitute for good clinical practice.) The records should be written when the clinical work is being done. Records prepared retrospectively in response to legal challenges or other allegations regarding our practice are generally not regarded favorably. Indeed the fact that they were not made when they should have been may be taken as evidence of poor practice.

How we should set about keeping records of interview material? Although interviews may be recorded on audiotape or videotape, and such records may be useful for certain purposes, there is no substitute for clear, permanent, written descriptions, or at least summaries, of our interviews.

Videotapes or audiotapes can be useful if the interviewer wishes to review the session in detail, and they also have applications for teaching and research. At first sight it might seem that a taped record of an interview, especially if it is on videotape, would also be the ideal permanent record, but in reality this is not so. Quite apart from the high cost of tapes and the amount of storage space that would be needed if all interviews were to be kept on tape indefinitely, there are other problems. Inevitably it takes as long to play a tape back as the original interview took. Only rarely do those who need to discover what happened in interviews have that sort of time available. On the other hand a written summary of an interview can be read in a few minutes at most. To summarize most interviews, though not necessarily those that aim to make a complete assessment of a young person's psychiatric or psychological status, one typed page or less, and two at most, is usually sufficient.

Preparing a written account of an interview is a useful exercise in itself. It is an opportunity for the interviewer to identify the main themes of the interview, summarize the content, and form an opinion of the significance of the material that emerged. The record should have three sections. The first should cover the purpose of the interview, who was present and whether anyone was watching, for example through a one-way observation screen. The middle section should describe the content of the interview, with a description of the subject's behavior and, if significant statements were made, quotations from what the subject said. The final section should state whether the interview's objectives were met and summarize the conclusions the interviewer has drawn from the session. In cases of suspected child abuse, a more detailed verbatim record of the child's significant statements should be included.

Should one take notes during interviews? The answer depends partly on the memory of the interviewer, partly on the nature of the interview. I usually take notes during initial assessment interviews; I explain that my memory is imperfect and that it is important to me that I have an accurate record of the facts I am learning during the interview, especially dates, time intervals and places. During initial assessment interviews I usually ask the child to help me prepare a genogram, unless he or she is too young to do it. This itself is a useful record and it is possible to write a lot of additional information on it as the child gives it to you.

Whether or not I take notes during the interview, I aim always to dictate my report or notes immediately after the interview ends. This means that my schedule must allow for the necessary time. Dictating immediately is ultimately a great time saver, at least for me, since I find it always easier and quicker to dictate a report when the interview is fresh in my mind than if I have to recall it later.

When an interview is conducted at the behest of a referring professional, the clinical record can sometimes take the form of a letter to the referrer. Whether this is feasible depends on how much detail of the interview it is appropriate to give to the particular referring person. This procedure can be a considerable time saver.

Penfold (1987) suggests that there are advantages, in many cases, to giving parents copies of psychiatric reports. She suggests that if such reports are written in constructive ways, this may be of benefit to the families. She recommends that pejorative terms such as overprotective, rejecting, inconsistent, immature, inadequate, abusive, and narcissistic be avoided when describing the behavior and characteristics of parents. Blaming the parents for their child's problems is seldom, if ever, helpful. Parenting is a "reciprocal and interactive process" and the emphasis of clinical reports should be on the child's needs and how these may be met, rather than on any perceived deficiencies of the parents.

"Open reporting," as Penfold (1987) calls her approach, is not the usual practice of most clinicians. She herself acknowledges that there are some cases in which the same report cannot be sent to the referring professional and to the parents. In others, if the report is appropriately written, it may be helpful to do so, though the child – if old enough to understand – should certainly be told what information will be included, and it is important not to break any confidences. There may sometimes be a case for letting the children concerned, and especially adolescents, see the reports concerning them.

How often should reports be made in a continuing series of interviews? This is a matter on which many counseling and therapy agencies have their own policies. I believe there should be at least a brief note on every interview, as well as on contacts made between interviews, for example, telephone conversations with clients, their families, their schools, or other people concerned. Typed rather than handwritten reports are much to be desired. It is therefore important to ensure that adequate secretarial assistance is available. To use the time of highly paid professionals writing records in longhand is generally uneconomic.

TAPING

If one is to videotape or audiotape an interview one must first obtain informed consent. If the child is old enough to give informed consent, he or she should be asked to give it, but the parent(s) or guardian should also agree. Whether the consent should be in writing depends on local practice and upon the law in the jurisdiction concerned. It may be sufficient to document in the clinical record that consent has been obtained, from whom, and after what explanation. The consent should also cover the uses that may be made of the tape recording. Another possibility is to record the consent on the tape.

Taping has the advantage that the interview can be studied in depth later. This can be useful for teaching interview and therapy skills. You can analyze a student's performance and give feedback concerning this on the basis of the recording. Some therapists find it useful to review their own interviews from time to time. This can help refine one's clinical skills. I find it can be useful when I find I am "stuck" in the treatment of a child or family. Taping is also necessary in some research studies which may use interview tapes to generate data.

The principal disadvantage of taping is that it may affect the behavior and responses of the child being interviewed. While a few of the more histrionic children like to perform before an audience or a camera, many tend to be inhibited by the idea that their every move and word are being recorded, or even that the conversation is being audiotaped. Careful preparation and discussion are therefore in order, and if possible it is better to delay taping interviews until rapport is well established.

Similar considerations apply to the observation of interviews through one-way screens. This also can be a valuable teaching or research procedure but it may adversely affect the process of the interview.

CONFIDENTIALITY

The limits of confidentiality have been discussed in Chapter 2. Here it is only necessary to point out that the security of clinical records is vital to achieving proper confidentiality. Clinical files should never be left unattended where unauthorized person may have access to them. When they are not in use they should be kept in a securely locked filing cabinet or storage room. Information should not be released without the proper consents, except where one is required by law to provide it.

LEGAL ISSUES

Consent to interview a child should always be obtained before the interview starts. When a child is brought in for interview by the parents or, if the parents are not the legal guardians, by the legal guardian, consent for the clinician to carry out the interview is implicit. In most jurisdictions it is probably unnecessary to seek a signed consent. It is sufficient to explain what you are about to do, answer any questions the parents or child may have, and document all this in the clinical record. When the child is brought in by someone without legal status, we should always try to contact the parents or guardian. Only in emergency situations in which delay might put the child at risk, is it advisable to proceed without consent. Some hospitals, agencies and other institutions have specific policies on consent, and these should always be followed.

The points discussed in Chapter 2 are of special relevance

when legal issues are involved. Questions of who the interview is being conducted for, what is to happen to the information obtained, and what are the limits of confidentiality may be crucial. Careful documentation is particularly important if reports may be required for court or if you may have to testify in court.

Interviews undertaken primarily for legal purposes, rather than for clinical ones, require special consideration. When you are asked to see children who are the subject of disputes between separating or divorcing parents, the permission of both parents, if both have legal status as guardians, is desirable. We should always obtain written permission of the legally responsible person(s) if the interview is being conducted on behalf of a third party, for example, a child welfare agency, a court or an insurance company.

Difficult decisions may need to be made in cases in which a parent is suspected of child abuse in any of its forms. Parents who have abused their children may be reluctant to give permission for their children to be interviewed. In such cases it is often wise to seek a further opinion from a consultant. It is usually important also to work in close liaison with the child welfare agency concerned.

From time to time it may be advisable to seek legal advice as to the proper course of action. This can often be obtained from professional associations and insurance companies providing malpractice protection or insurance. They are likely to be better informed on these issues than your neighborhood family lawyer.

SUMMARY

The termination of a series of interviews requires careful planning and sensitive handling. Saying goodbye to a therapist or counselor after a long period of contact can provoke feelings of loss, sadness, and even rejection, and these must be dealt with as part of the termination process. Similar consideration apply to interruptions to a series of interviews.

Keeping accurate and up-to-date records of clinical interviews is a basic feature of good clinical practice. It is necessary for both clinical and legal purposes. Notes and reports should be typed wherever possible and should be made, or ideally dictated, immediately after the interview. Videotapes or audiotapes are seldom satisfactory as permanent records, but have value for teaching, learning, and research purposes. The confidentiality of records must be assured at all times.

Proper consent from the child's parents or legal guardian should always be obtained before a child is interviewed. Special considerations apply to interviews which serve a legal, rather than primarily clinical, purpose.

REFERENCES

Ainsworth, M., Blehar, M., Waters, E., & Walls, S. (1978). *Patterns of attachment*. Hillsdale, NJ: Lawrence Erlbaum.

Alford, J. D. & Locke, B. J. (1984). Clinical responses to psychopathology of mentally retarded persons. *American Journal of Mental Deficiency, 89*, 195–197.

American Psychiatric Association (1987). *Diagnostic and statistical manual of mental disorders* (3rd ed. – Revised). Washington, DC: A.P.A.

Anderson, K. A. (1971). The "shopping" behavior of parents of mentally retarded children; the professional person's role. *Mental Retardation, 9*, 3–5.

Bandler, R. & Grinder, J. (1979). *Frogs into princes*. Moab, Utah: Real People Press.

Bandler, R., Grinder, J., & Satir, V. (1976). *Changing with families*. Palo Alto: Science and Behavior Books.

Barker, P. (1986). *Basic family therapy*, (2nd ed.). Oxford: Blackwell; New York: Oxford.

Barker, P. (1988). *Basic child psychiatry*, (5th ed.). Oxford: Blackwell; Chicago: Year Book.

Barker, P. (in press). The psychiatric examination of children with emotional and behavioural difficulties. In *The management of children with emotional and behavioural difficulties*, edited by V. Varma. London: Routledge.

Bayley, N. (1969). *Bayley scales of infant development: Birth to two years*. New York: Psychological Corporation.

Blum, K. (1984). *Handbook of abusable drugs*. New York: Gardner Press.

Bowie, David. (1970). All the madmen. From the album *The man who sold the world*. Mercury 61325.

Bowlby, J. (1977). The making and breaking of emotional bonds. *British Journal of Psychiatry, 130*, 201–210 and 421–431.

Bowlby, J. (1988). Developmental psychiatry comes of age. *American Journal of Psychiatry, 145*, 1–10.

Bierman, K. L. & Schwartz, L. A. (1986). Clinical child interviews: approaches and developmental considerations. *Journal of Child and Adolescent Psychotherapy, 3*, 267–278.

Brown, B. & Lloyd, H. (1975). A controlled study of children not speaking at school. *Journal of the Association of Workers for Maladjusted Children, 3*, 49–63.

Chess, S. & Thomas, A. (1984). *Origins and evolution of behavior disorders from infancy to early adult life*. New York: Brunner/Mazel.

Creative Therapeutics (1973). The talking, feeling and doing game. (Available from Creative Therapeutics, 155 County Road, Cresskill, New Jersey 07626.)

Dent, H. R. (1986). An experimental study of the effectiveness of different techniques of questioning mentally handicapped witnesses. *British Journal of Clinical Psychology, 25,* 13–17.

Dent, H. R. & Stephenson, G. M. (1979). An experimental study of the effectiveness of different techniques of questioning child witnesses. *British Journal of Clinical Psychology, 18,* 41–51.

DiLeo, J. H. (1983). *Interpreting children's drawings.* New York: Brunner/Mazel.

Dilts, R., Grinder, J., Bandler, R., Bandler, L. C., & DeLozier, J. (1980). *Neuro-linguistic programming (Vol. 1).* Cupertino, CA: Meta Publications.

Erickson, M. H., Hershman, S., & Sector, I. I. (1961). *The practical application of medical and dental hypnosis.* Chicago: Seminars on Hypnosis Publishing Co.

Esman, A. H. (1988). Assessment of the adolescent. In *Handbook of clinical assessment of children and adolescents (Vol. 1),* edited by C. J. Kestenbaum & D. T. Williams. New York: Universities Press.

Fisch, G. S., Cohen, I. L., Wolf, E. G., Brown, W. T., Jenkins, E. C., & Gross, A. (1986). Autism and the fragile X syndrome. *American Journal of Psychiatry, 143,* 71–73.

Gaensbauer, T. J. & Harmon, R. J. (1981). Clinical assessment in infancy utilizing structured playroom situations. *Journal of the American Academy of Child Psychiatry, 20,* 264–280.

Garbarino, J., Guttman, E., & Seeley, J. W. (1986). *The psychologically battered child.* San Francisco: Jossey-Bass.

Gilberg, C. & Wahlstrom, J. (1985). Chromosome abnormalities in infantile autism and other childhood psychoses. *Developmental Medicine and Child Neurology, 27,* 293–304.

Harlow H. F. (1958) The nature of love. *American Journal of Psychology, 13,* 673–685.

Hawton, K., O'Grady, J., Osborn, M., & Cole, D. (1982). Adolescents who take overdoses: Their characteristics, problems and contacts with helping agencies. *British Journal of Psychiatry, 140,* 118–123.

Helfer, R. E. & Kempe, R. F. (Eds.) (1987). *The battered child* (4th ed.). University of Chicago Press.

Jones, D. P. H. & McQuiston, M. G. (1988). *Interviewing the sexually abused child* (3rd ed.). London: Gaskell.

Karpel, M. A. & Strauss, E. S. (1983). *Family evaluation.* New York: Gardner Press.

Knobloch, H. & Pasaminick, B. (1974). *Gesell and Amatruda's developmental diagnosis.* Hagerstown, MD: Harper & Row.

Kolvin, I. & Fundudis, T. (1981). Electively mute children: psychological development and background factors. *Journal of Child Psychology and Psychiatry, 22,* 219–232

Lankton, S. R. & Lankton, C. (1983). *The answer within.* New York: Brunner/Mazel.

Menolascino, F. J., Gilson, S. F., & Levitas, A. S. (1986). Issues in the treatment of mentally retarded patients in the community mental health system. *Community Mental Health Journal, 22*, 314–327.

Minde, K. & Minde, R. (1986). *Infant psychiatry: An introductory textbook*. Beverly Hills: Sage.

Minuchin, S. (1974). *Families and family therapy*. Cambridge, Mass: Harvard University Press.

Myers, K. M., Burke, P., & McCauley, E. (1985). Suicidal behavior by hospitalized preadolescent children on a psychiatric unit. *Journal of the American Academy of Child Psychiatry, 24*, 474–480.

Offer, D., Ostrov, E., & Howard, K. (1981). The mental health professional's concept of the normal adolescent. *Archives of General Psychiatry, 38*, 149–152.

Offer, D. & Offer, J. (1975). Three developmental routes through male adolescence. *Adolescent Psychiatry, 4*, 121–141.

Penfold, P. S. (1987). Open reporting in child psychiatry. *Canadian Journal of Psychiatry, 32*, 761–763.

Pfeffer, C. R., Zuckerman, S., Plutchkin, R., & Mizruchi, M. S. (1984). Suicidal behaviour in normal school children. *Journal of the American Academy of Child Psychiatry, 23*, 416–423.

Provence, S., Leonard, M. & Naylor, A. (1982). Developmental diagnosis: An approach to assessing mental health in infants. Presented at the Congress of the International Association for Child and Adolescent Psychiatry and Allied Professions, Dublin, Ireland.

Rich, J. (1968). *Interviewing children and adolescents*. London: Macmillan.

Rossi, E. L. (1985). *Dreams and the growth of personality*. New York: Brunner/Mazel

Rutter, M. (1975). Psychiatric disorder and intellectual impairment in childhood. *British Journal of Hospital Medicine, 8*, 137–140.

Rutter, M. & Cox, A. (1981) Psychiatric interviewing techniques: I. Methods and measures. *British Journal of Psychiatry, 138*, 273–282.

Rutter, M., Graham, P., Chadwick, O., & Yule, W. (1976). Adolescent turmoil: fact or fiction? *Journal of Child Psychology and Psychiatry, 17*, 35–56.

Shaffer, D. (1974). Suicide in childhood and adolescence. *Journal of Child Psychology and Psychiatry, 15*, 275–291.

Shaw, J. A. & Budd, E. C. (1982). Determinants of acquiescence and naysaying of mentally retarded persons. *American Journal of Mental Deficiency, 87*, 108–110.

Sigelman, C. K., Budd, E. C., Spanhel, C. L., & Schoenrock, C. J. (1981a). When in doubt say yes: Acquiscence in interviews with mentally retarded persons. *Mental Retardation, 19*, 53–58.

Sigelman, C. K., Budd, E. C., Spanhel, C. L., & Schoenrock, C. J. (1981b). Asking questions of retarded persons: A comparison of yes-no and either-or formats. *Applied Research in Mental Retardation, 2*, 347–357.

Sigelman, C. K., Budd, E. C., Winer, J. L., Schoenrock, C. J., & Martin, P. W. (1982). Evaluating alternative techniques of questioning mentally retarded persons. *American Journal of Mental Deficiency, 86*, 511–518.

Spengler, O. (1926). *The decline of the west* (Vol. 1, abridged), page 166. New York: Alfred A. Knopf.

Walker, L. E. A. (Ed.). (1988). *Handbook of sexual abuse of children*. New York: Springer.

White, S., Strom, G. A., Santilli, G. & Halpin, B. M. (1986). Interviewing young sexual abuse victims with anatomically correct dolls. *Child Abuse and Neglect, 10*, 519–529.

NAME INDEX

Ainsworth, M., 74, 155
Alford, J. D., 93, 155
American Psychiatric Association, 130, 134, 155
Anderson, K. A., 93, 155

Bandler, L. C., 33, 156
Bandler, R., 33, 155, 156
Barker, P., 1, 18, 22, 46, 47, 68, 105, 130, 134, 135, 136, 138, 141, 155
Bayley, N., 84, 155
Blehar, M., 74, 155
Blum, K., 60, 138, 155
Bowie, D., 88, 155
Bowlby, J., 74, 81, 155
Bierman, K. L., 3, 155
Brown, B., 133, 155
Brown, W. T., 131, 156
Budd, E. C., 102, 157
Burke, P., 126, 157

Chadwick, O., 50, 157
Chess, S., 86, 155
Cohen, I. L., 131, 156
Cole, D., 125, 156
Cox, A., 8, 10, 157
Creative Therapeutics, 69, 155

DeLozier, J., 33, 156
Dent, H. R., 103, 156
DiLeo, J. H., 45, 156
Dilts, R., 33, 156

Erickson, M. H., 7, 156
Esman, A. H., 55, 156

Fisch, G. S., 131, 156
Fundudis, T., 133, 156

Gaensbauer, T. J., 84, 156
Garbarino, J., 105, 116, 156
Gilberg, C., 131, 156
Gilson, S. F., 93, 156
Graham, P., 50, 157
Grinder, J., 33, 156
Gross, A., 131, 156
Guttman, E., 105, 156

Halpin, B. M., 115, 158
Harlow, H. F., 81, 156
Harmon, R. J., 84, 156
Hawton, K., 125, 156
Helfer, R. E., 105, 156
Hershman, S., 7, 156
Howard, K., 50, 157

Jenkins, E. C., 131, 156
Jones, D. P. H., 105, 114, 115, 156

Karpel, M. A., 31, 156
Kempe, R. F., 105, 156
Kestenbaum, C. J., 156
Knobloch, H., 85, 156
Kolvin, I., 133, 156

Lankton, C., 142, 156
Lankton, S. R., 142, 156
Leonard, M., 85, 157
Levitas, A. S., 93, 156
Locke, B. J., 93, 155
Lloyd, H., 133, 155

Martin, P. W., 102, 157
McCauley, E., 126, 157
McQuiston, M. G., 105, 114, 115, 156
Menolascino, F. J., 93, 156
Minde, K., 83, 84, 85, 157

SUBJECT INDEX